Pacific Saints

Their Battles for Eternity

Blessings,
Joe

Plessinger,
Joe

Joe Gervais

Pacific Saints

Their Battles for Eternity

Dedication

To Susan, my love – you have encouraged me every step of the way – when it has been easy and when it has been extremely difficult. I love you.

Acknowledgements

To Joyce Wilson and Mary Ann Maring, who brought Susan and me to our first Wycliffe Associates Banquet – that invitation was the critical first step towards Susan and me serving with Wycliffe Associates today.

The people profiled in the book are just a small portion of the amazing team God has assembled for the work in the Pacific. There was no way for me to profile everyone, but all your contributions are essential to this body fulfilling the mission. The team is growing like a megachurch and it grieves me that I can no longer build and maintain relationships with everyone involved. There's also the team I left behind in South Asia. There are Dan's minions. All are part of this story. Wycliffe Associates is registered as a church, and the associates are an amazing portion of the Body of Christ – the staff in Orlando, my partners in the development team raising funds for all this work, the volunteers, many of whom have served alongside me in different parts of the world at their own expense.

Behind the scenes Tabitha Price, Jean Spall, and Ginger Wilkinson helped edit the book and correct my grammar to proper American English. There was also a team of readers that gave me feedback on early drafts. Thank you.

Contents

Foreword
By Bruce A. Smith

Have you ever prayed for a miracle?

One of the miracles I've prayed for is that every person on earth would have access to the Bible in their first language—their heart language. For some of you this will seem an odd prayer. We've got dozens of Bible versions on our shelves and on our phones. It's easy to imagine that everyone in the world has the same experience. Unfortunately, that is not the case.

In a day in which there are more mobile devices than people in the world, God's Word is still inaccessible to too many. At this point in world history, fewer than 700 languages have the complete Bible. Perhaps this number sounds high to you, but for hundreds of millions of people worldwide this means they have little or no Scripture in their heart language—and they are discouraged.

"Why doesn't anyone care about us?" I've faced this question too many times. When Scripture is available in neighboring languages, but not in their own language, the people get the message loud and clear. "You're not worth the effort." That is likely not the message we intend to communicate, but our inaction speaks louder than our words.

Into this challenge, God has drawn Joe and Susan Gervais.

I have had the privilege of walking alongside Joe and Susan for most of this past decade as God has drawn them into Bible translation. I remember meeting them at one of our events in California. Joe was

Chair of their church's Missions Committee and already familiar with Bible translation through supporting several missionary families.

Not long after that, Joe and Susan moved from California to Vermont to care for Susan's mom. My wife, Jan, and I traveled to Vermont to stay connected to Joe and Susan. Early one morning I came upon Joe reading his Bible and taking notes. As he finished writing, I asked him a question. "Would you be interested in using your spare time to help create free resources for national Bible translators worldwide?" Joe passed on that opportunity. A short time later, Joe and Susan joined as Wycliffe Associates volunteers facilitating MAST.

Joe's first step of faith led to more steps of faith. God was miraculously stirring dozens, then hundreds, of language groups ready, willing, and able to begin Bible translation in their languages. Joe accepted an invitation to support a few of these national translators with training and technology. I often say that at Wycliffe Associates the reward for doing good work is the opportunity to do more. That describes Joe's experience here. God kept opening doors, and Joe kept stepping through by faith.

Joe had a second chance to help with the resources for national translators when he shared in coordinating teams to translate these resources into 39 major languages so that anyone bilingual in those languages can now benefit from them. Joe has trained and served several hundred Bible translators, enabling them to launch and accelerate Bible translation in their own languages. He's also been instrumental in recruiting and developing hundreds of additional Bible translation trainers and engaging dozens of church leaders throughout the South Pacific and Asia. Their vision is to launch Bible translation in more than 1000 languages in the coming year!

Those of you who know Joe may begin to have some sense of the miracle God is doing within Joe to accomplish these things through Joe.

Foreword

In the pages that follow, you'll hear more of the ways that God is moving to make Himself known to the nations. The essence of this story is that God is preparing, calling, and empowering THOUSANDS of people worldwide to get His Word translated into every language — so that every person can know Jesus Christ as Lord and Savior! You'll get to know some of these dear brothers and sisters in Christ in the coming pages.

The fact that Joe and Susan are part of this story reflects how God often chooses to work miraculously — first within us, then through us.

Astronaut Jim Lovell once said, "There are people who make things happen, people who watch things happen, and people who wonder what happened. To be successful you need to be a person who makes things happen."

You, too, can be a part of this story. Take a step of faith.

Preface

Pacific Saints: Their Battles for Eternity is a memoir of my journey to a personal relationship with Jesus Christ and the Holy Spirit and my abandonment of the easy money of Silicon Valley for the vast riches of working to build His Kingdom.

On October 24, 2019, I boarded a flight from Nadi, Fiji, to Hong Kong. This was the first of nine mostly long-haul flights I would take over the next eight days to travel to Indonesia, back to Fiji, and back to America, including four overnight redeye flights.

During a quiet moment at the start of this brutal nine days of travel between these countries, while reading a book about Sabbath (Allender, 2010), the Holy Spirit suddenly gave me this book. It was like an instantaneous high-speed movie running through my head. As He did, I started weeping in gratitude, not just for the divine inspiration, but for all the glorious chapters and the brothers and sisters in Christ I have the privilege of serving and serving alongside.

Pacific Saints will take you from the waning years before the death of my life as a marketing professional in the computer industry, to the glorious life I live now, serving the King of Kings as a shepherd, king, and priest, doing the absolute impossible, that is so far beyond human comprehension that I just stand in awe at the loving God I serve.

Some are skeptical about what we are doing, serving God to eliminate biblical poverty worldwide, ensuring every tongue, nation, language, and people have complete Bibles by the year 2025. *Pacific Saints* highlights the miraculous team of national leaders God has assembled for His task. I have the privilege of serving Him through serving these Pacific saints in pursuing this vision.

Pacific Saints will carry you through who these saints are, how God called them, and the battles they are fighting to transform their nations for eternity.

Enjoy!

Joe

Section One

Therefore, if anyone is in Christ, he is a new creation. The old has passed away; behold, the new has come. All this is from God, who through Christ reconciled us to himself and gave us the ministry of reconciliation.[1]

---

[1] 2 Corinthians 5:17-18

Chapter One – It's all meaningless – or is it?
The Early Years

I was born in Rhode Island in the early sixties, the oldest of four children. Through my teen years I had both sets of grandparents living and two great-grandfathers. I remember things always being difficult with my father's parents and much easier with my mother's parents. I'd frequently spend time with my maternal grandfather. He was a big sports fan and spent many years involved in Little League Baseball. What a disappointment I must have been unable to hit the side of a barn with my swing, but I remember the patience Gramps exhibited as he taught me to catch a baseball and swing a golf putter.

In my younger years my grandparents had a few acres and Gramps always had a nice flower garden and a great vegetable garden. He raised chickens and rabbits. That's how I got my love of growing things. My interest in building things ran deep in my genes from both sides of my family. While Gramps built his modest house after World War II, my Pépère, or great-grandfather on my father's side, was a prolific inventor and had many, many stories.

Pépère lived to be 100 years old, so I enjoyed visiting with him until my early 20s. He was born in Quebec and immigrated to the United States as a teen. I remember as he aged, we would talk and sometimes the conversation would become difficult. He'd explain that he couldn't think in English any longer. Since I didn't speak French, he would have to translate what I was saying into French, think about it, then translate a response back to English so I could understand. Little did I know how relevant this experience would be four decades later as I moved into full-time ministry. Today, from the experience with my great-grandfather, I know the importance of heart language. I also know that decades using a second language does not replace the mother tongue.

One of my ancestors, Benedict Arnold, was part of the first 13 families that settled the Providence Plantation, the first Governor of Rhode Island, and a member of the First Baptist Church in America, founded in 1638 and known as the First Baptist Church of Providence. All my immediate ancestors were Roman Catholics – my parents, my grandparents, the great-grandparents I knew. I did all the things you do as a Catholic – baptism as a baby, first communion, and confirmation. This upbringing gave me a view of God as a punishing God, where if I wasn't good, I was going to hell. It also taught me separation from God – everything was done through a priest. I wasn't taught that I could just cry out to God as David did in many of the Psalms. I couldn't go directly to God in repentance, I did it through a priest in a confessional.

I mentioned my parents' relationship with my dad's parents being difficult. As I matured, I recognized a pattern of emotional abuse that spanned generations. My father was the oldest of five sons and was blamed throughout the years for many things that weren't his fault, for example being blamed for his next youngest brother's issues. There were also hurtful comments directed at my mom from her father-in-law. This pattern was repeated in my relationship with my dad. While I wasn't necessarily being blamed for things, certain statements were etched into me. For example, as I was graduating high school at sixteen my dad told me that I'd never amount to anything. While he was trying to use reverse psychology, it created hurts I carried for years; and this learned behavior impacted how I interacted with my sons, particularly my older son Jonathan. My dad wasn't unique in making these statements. I recently found that my friend John had the same statements made by his father when he was a teen.

After high school, I started studying computer science in college. My high school math teacher, Mr. Clark, was an Army Reservist and motivated me to join the Army's Simultaneous Membership Program, where I'd be both a reservist and a Reserve Officer's Training Corps (ROTC) cadet. Having graduated at sixteen, I couldn't join the army until a few weeks later when I turned seventeen. The day after my birthday, I was off to Basic Training at Fort Leonard Wood, Missouri. I started college at Syracuse University immediately after Basic Training.

College was a juggle of classes, part-time work, ROTC, and my reserve commitment. I was advised to delay my entry into the ROTC advanced program a year. During my first year of college I was a normal reservist. The summer before my sophomore year I attended military occupation specialty (MOS) school as a clerk typist at Fort Jackson, South Carolina. I then moved to California for my sophomore year of college. This reunited me with my family, who had moved during my freshman year. At San Jose State I continued ROTC and kept up my computer science studies at California State University at Hayward (now California State East Bay). Before my 20th birthday I found myself a butter bar – a Second Lieutenant in the United States Army. For years I joked that it took an act of Congress to make me into a gentleman, and I have the paper to prove it – my commissioning certificate. Today I know that to be a gentleman, I need a deep, intimate, and personal relationship with Jesus Christ, and even with that, there are still days I come up short; but I no longer must wait for confession on Saturday night to set things right.

I ultimately spent just shy of 10 years in the Army Reserves and California Army National Guard. While I commanded a small detachment towards the end of this stint, I always questioned my leadership – never feeling like the hard-charging military leaders portrayed in the movies.

Walking Away from Religion
I finished my undergraduate degree before my 21st birthday. Being the underachiever my father always told me I would become, in a two-week period I graduated, started my first full-time professional job, got

married, and signed a lease-to-own contract on my first home. It was a busy June.

The wedding had one of those moments etched deeply in my story. The hierarchy of church leadership in the Catholic Church – from priests to bishops to cardinals to the Pope – had been made clear to me. I was raised that priests were better than me and in better standing with God due to their role. As I was waiting for the ceremony to begin, I was standing with two of my friends in the wedding party and my two younger brothers. This is when Father Crawford approached me and told me to "Get those assholes to church" as he referred to my two brothers. While nowhere near as hurtful as the abuse that others faced as part of the Catholic Church's sexual scandal, it was still hurtful to me.

> *"If anyone considers himself religious and does not keep a tight rein on his tongue, he deceives himself and his religion is worthless."*[2]

My first wife and I did attend church the first few years of our marriage and had both our sons baptized after their births, but over time we drifted from the church.

Initially unbeknownst to me, she replaced church with a methamphetamine addiction. Addiction is a cunning and baffling disease. While she and I were dating, there were a couple things I set boundaries around – smoking and drugs. In hindsight, I was a bit controlling during that period. I can remember a couple times – once while dating and once 8-10 years into my marriage – where I snapped in anger. I'm not proud of those outbursts. After the second one there was a deep scar in the stainless kitchen sink from a Pyrex saucepan that got the brunt of my rage and served as a reminder of that outburst the rest of the time we lived in that house.

------

[2] James 1:26

Chapter One

As I look at that marriage, there were a number of challenges in it. We were just getting settled into the marriage when I got a call at work that her mother was dead. I thought this was a joke, but soon discovered she had been brutally murdered. For years my mother-in-law's estranged husband was under a cloud of suspicion, but it wasn't until decades later that DNA results cleared him and revealed the identity of the killer.[3]

I attended my officer basic course at Fort Gordon, Georgia, the spring following her mom's death. That fall I started on a graduate degree, just over a year after we were married. Three and a half years of night school later I completed my Master of Business Administration. Within a couple months of graduation, our first son, Jonathan, was born. He was five weeks early and a little small, struggling with jaundice in his first few weeks, but started thriving quickly. At six months old he had his first bout with asthma. This would be a lifelong struggle for him, but in his first six years we faced many hospitalizations – from a few days to weeks at a time – and he also became steroid dependent. This was a real challenge because the prednisone helped his asthma significantly, yet he was starting to show bone density issues from the prolonged use of the steroid.

One thing I learned in the struggles with Jonathan's asthma was that even though it was bad and scary, it probably wouldn't kill him. On more than one occasion, he was at the Children's Hospital at Stanford University in a ward with many patients with Cystic Fibrosis, which at the time was typically fatal. This helped us to keep perspective on Jonathan's disease.

Alexander followed Jonathan's arrival by 14 months. The two boys couldn't be more different, but they both brought a lot of joy to the

---

3   https://www.latimes.com/socal/daily-pilot/news/tn-dpt-xpm-2008-11-13-dpt-pipeline111408-story.html

household. I lost the naming battle for Alexander – getting his middle name Andrew, but we called him Andy around the house. He had some struggles with asthma, such as on his first Christmas when he had an attack as we took home the Christmas tree – a tree that never made it in the house and led to many years of artificial trees.

Andy was always going – always on the move as a kid. I remember his first trip to Europe when he was about seven years old. We were visiting a museum in Belgium. He told me I was going too fast through the museum, then proceeded to sit in front of a 15th century oil painting on wood and studied it like he was watching TV for the next 15 minutes.

School was a challenge for Andy. He used his first name at school – Alex – which allowed him to leave the bullying of school and come home and be Andy. We spent many years trying to figure out why he was having difficulty; and, finally, when he was eleven years old he was diagnosed with a high functioning form of autism, known at the time as Asperger's Syndrome. People with Asperger's can be very smart but have major challenges understanding social cues and can tend to see the world in black and white.

After our tenth anniversary, there was a four-year period of increased craziness around the house – delusions, crazy sleeping patterns, inconsistencies. During that period my first wife started seeing a psychiatrist. She was diagnosed with bipolar disorder, but what I found out later was that she was also self-medicating with stimulants and alcohol. The medical professionals figured it out much earlier than I did. It shouldn't have been a surprise to me given the history of alcoholism in her family; but like many others facing addiction, I was in a state of denial. It all came to a head in the spring of 1998 when she had a blackout. The next morning when she went to her psychiatrist appointment, she ended up being admitted to a detox, where she had over a 0.5 blood alcohol content. Casual drinkers don't see those kind of numbers, only chronic alcoholics.

As she was in her first rehab, I found the rooms of the Al-Anon Family Groups for friends and families of alcoholics. My boys also started attending a pre-teen program for children affected by someone's drinking. While I came in to the rooms of Al-Anon with a lot of anger and hurt, today I can say that I'm grateful for the alcoholic, because Al-Anon changed my life and led me to a personal relationship with Jesus Christ.

We continued the dance with alcohol and drug addiction over the next six years. Four years into that merry-go-round, after my first wife had another stint in rehab and a halfway house, I made the decision that I didn't want to share my marriage with methamphetamines any more. Was I necessarily a good detective when Mr. Addiction moved back in? No. It took several months to figure it out.

It took me a few years in Al-Anon to work a focused program on my own personal recovery. As we change, the relationship with the alcoholic changes. I started doing more with friends in the program, and I started working the 12 steps with a sponsor. Through this personal reflection, I saw the position of my older son. Much of the family focus was on his mother and her addiction, and what wasn't there was on his brother and his autism. Jonathan was burdened with unreasonable responsibility as a child because of his mother's condition and just didn't get a fair shake. This took me a long time to see.

In 2003 Jonathan and I went to Reno in my Corvette as part of the 50th Anniversary Bash Corvette Caravan back to Bowling Green, Kentucky. I had made the whole run to Bowling Green in 1999 with a friend, but this time we just did the first leg. At dinner that night I asked how I could be a better dad, but Jonathan couldn't really give me an answer.

A couple months later Jonathan and I went to an Alateen fundraiser – a campout at Lake Mendocino. I was hobbling that weekend, having torn the meniscus in my knee and awaiting surgery to repair it. I remember at the campfire some of the teens were sharing about emotional abuse and it just cut to the core. At that point it was crystal clear that Jonathan was yet the next generation suffering from emotional abuse as a child, just as I had experienced and my dad had experienced before me. It was time to break the cycle, and Al-Anon was giving me the tools. That weekend also expanded my circle of friends in the program.

In Al-Anon there were several conferences and other events. Jonathan and I attended a conference in the Redwoods, the Growing Together Weekend in Occidental, California, in the spring of 2004. Some old friends helped me take the blinders off that weekend as to some of the risk to my kids in my household. I also remember taking a hike with a group of people up to a wooden cross on the top of a hill. I was talking with a woman and we were having a great conversation. I remember at the end of the hike praying, "God, if only I could talk to my wife like that." It was always difficult talking with my wife. Addiction is a cunning and baffling disease, and it stunts emotional maturity, usually stopping emotional growth at the point the person succumbs to addiction. I struggled in Al-Anon because I had female friends that I could have deeper conversations with than I could have with my wife. This set off bells and warning lights.

About six weeks after the weekend in Occidental with Jonathan, it was clear that methamphetamine was ruling the household again. There were a number of small accidents with our truck. I also learned that Jonathan, unlicensed and 15 years old, was being asked to drive the truck and pick up his brother from school – 35 miles away – because his mother was too inebriated to drive. On the eve of our twentieth wedding anniversary I decided enough was enough. I wrote a letter to her, taking responsibility for my part in our brokenness. I shared the letter with my sponsor; fortunately, he was able to read it and respond before he had to leave for the airport for a trip to Europe.

My biggest mistake in the divorce was trying to have an amicable divorce and sharing the house during the process. If I didn't want the disease in the house, why was I letting the disease still stay in the house? Finding empty bags of drugs during that period confirmed that stupidity.

I could tell a lot more of my back story, but the one thing I will say is none of it was wasted. All of it plays into who I am today. All of it has prepared me for the journey I am on with the ministry I serve today.

The Lord has made everything for its purpose, even the wicked for the day of trouble.[4]

---

[4] Proverbs 16:4

Chapter Two – Susan, My Love

Do not let your adorning be external — the braiding of hair and the putting on of gold jewelry, or the clothing you wear — but let your adorning be the hidden person of the heart with the imperishable beauty of a gentle and quiet spirit, which in God's sight is very precious.[5]

The Walk

In the previous chapter I talked about a hike I took at Occidental with an unnamed woman and praying after the hike to be able to have the ease of conversation I had with her with my wife. God answered that prayer but only after divorce. And it turns out the love of my life is the woman I was hiking with that day.

Susan will have to write her own story, but from the time we first met at the Bash at Lake Mendicino, we kept running into each other at Al-Anon and Alateen events and enjoyed being around each other. Neither of us had a physical attraction to each other, but we shared a certain ease and comfort. I was not Susan's type – I wasn't tall and I certainly wasn't thin, weighing 275 pounds at the time. Nevertheless, God kept on having our paths intersect.

Shortly after filing for divorce in the summer of 2004, I took Jonathan and several other teens from Northern California to Washington State for an Alateen conference. My coworkers thought I was nuts to be cooped up in a car round trip to Washington, but it was a lot of fun. Susan went with me as a second chaperone. We stopped overnight at my sister's house outside Portland, Oregon, on the way up and the way back from Washington.

---

[5] 1 Peter 3:3-4

My friend Cathy was at the Washington event. I talked with her about Susan. Cathy thought we were already dating and had a conversation with Susan. Today we call Cathy our matchmaker. At my sister's house, Susan told me some of her boundaries. Her Al-Anon program was very important to her, and one of her rules was not to date anyone in the program. That lasted less than a week after we returned from Oregon. My mom had recently had knee surgery, and I asked Susan if she wanted to go with me to visit my parents that following weekend. She had met my parents when we had stopped at the hospital on the way to Washington following my mom's surgery.

At the time Susan and I started dating, it was in a worldly manner. While Susan didn't move in because she ran a housecleaning business 75 miles away from my home, we frequently spent weekends together, depending on who had custody of their kids that weekend. Susan's older son Chad married a month after we started dating. At ages 16, 15, and 14, Susan's son Travis and my sons Jonathan and Alexander were still finishing high school.

Forgoing Sin

As we started dating, we both were growing in our faith. About a year and a half before we started dating I had started attending an evangelical Christian church that a number of my Al-Anon friends attended. Susan was also looking for a church near her home. Over time, Susan more frequently attended church with me, particularly after I got full custody of my boys.

Crash Course in Learning to Pray

Growing in faith and dating in a worldly way cause tension. Susan and I had been dating for a little over a year, and we decided to go camping for her birthday at Big Basin State Park in the coastal redwood forest of the Santa Cruz mountains. I think this is one of the first times as I look back that I really can say I was following the leading of the Holy Spirit.

We were having an intense conversation as we frequently did. After years of not being able to have great conversations with my wife, I was starving for those conversations. Shortly before we arrived at the park, I asked that dreaded question: did Susan regret us being physically intimate? Why I asked that question, I'm still not sure. That I asked it while driving really wasn't a smart move, but I did, and once I did, I couldn't un-ask the question. Unbeknownst to me, Susan had been wrestling with the answer to that question for days, maybe even weeks.

As we talked further, Susan shared how she had been seeking counsel of friends and was really wrestling with growing as a Christian and being intimate outside of marriage. She had planned to tell me that she couldn't continue like that anymore and was willing to take the consequences of that decision, whether it meant I would stay in the relationship or not. She honestly didn't think I would stay in the relationship.

We officially began our vow of celibacy on the spot. The following night there was an Al-Anon function back at home, so we drove the hour back from the mountains and attended the function. One of our church elders was there, so we confessed to him and he lifted us up in prayer. We were engaged at that time but had not yet set a wedding date. Two weeks would have been a long time to wait, but we ended up setting a date over the Christmas holidays for the following Thanksgiving weekend.

That 54 weeks between the start of the vow of celibacy and the wedding was a challenging time. The desire did not subside one bit. Anytime the desire became too strong, we did the only thing we could – we got on our knees and prayed. We developed a lot of callouses on our knees, but we were able to get much closer and deal with issues we needed to clean up.

Financial Freedom

"Or how can you say to your brother, 'Let me take the speck out of your eye,' when there is the log in your own eye?"[6]

As Susan and I were dating and practicing our vow of celibacy, one of the things we did was examine the financial carnage in each of our situations. Susan's sole proprietorship kept food on the table and paid the rent on a basic two-bedroom apartment but didn't cover luxuries like medical insurance.

One weekend that we were together I asked if she minded if we pulled up her credit report. As we were going through it, I realized that her consumer debt basically amounted to her annual income. She was way over her head, with no margin to get out of that mess. Not yet having been introduced to Dave Ramsey and his principles, I convinced Susan to let me take out a zero-interest signature loan to help her get ahead of the problem. I hadn't learned that debt is a heart issue, not a math problem.

It took me a few days to come to the awareness that I was no better off than Susan with my non-mortgage debt. At the time, I was making roughly around five times what Susan was making a year, and lo and behold, had car loan and credit card debt matching my income. I just wasn't seeing it at first, because my income was so much bigger than Susan's. I had to confess to Susan that my situation was just as unmanageable.

Greed drove some of my debt and enabling the rest. At the time I was working for a Silicon Valley startup. Stock options are a big part of the startup environment. In my divorce, I didn't want to give up any of my stock options to my soon to be ex-wife, nor did I want to part with the majority of my retirement account. Someday I will frame the stock

---

[6] Matthew 7:4

certificates, which today are just worthless wallpaper, with the company defunct.

I gave my ex-wife the newer vehicle, a less than two-year-old pickup truck, and kept the loan for it. I also kept all the consumer debt, because my ex-wife wasn't working, having been a stay-at-home mom while our kids were younger. So I kept the debt and let her walk away with free and clear assets. She had a degree in early childhood education, but it's hard to make a career in that field when you're using drugs and in and out of rehab. As I look back, even in divorce I was enabling and making things easier on her for the short term but not helping in the long term.

Starting to clean up the debt was also one of my first big lessons in surrender – my ex-wife got the newer Chevy pickup, I kept the older Suburban and the three hotrods, because everyone needs three hotrods. Okay, everyone needs two hotrods and a dedicated race car. In the months leading up to the wedding, I surrendered the classic 1969 Chevy Camaro that was my ex-wife's first car. With hotrods, they are never done, only doing, and I had been building that car for over 20 years since 1983. It was in the final stages of the second restoration since we had the car. I also had a 1988 Chevy Corvette that was a dedicated race car for Open Road Racing – basically time distance rally races run on closed public highways at 2-3 times the posted speed limit.

Knowing that selling things is one way to eliminate debt, I decided to surrender these two cars; and I surrendered them to God, admitting it was time to let them go. I posted on an email group with my car buddies that I was going to sell Red, the race car. Shortly after that, my friend Scott asked if I was going to sell Cormaro (the Camaro, nicknamed because it had a 4th generation Corvette front suspension on it and an electronic fuel injected LT1 engine under the hood with matching 4L60E transmission). Within hours I had an agreement to sell Scott the car for $20,000.

Though negotiating the sale was easy, the car didn't go easy. The day of the sale I drove it to my office, and Scott was going to meet me at lunchtime. We were doing the paperwork for the sale on the roof of the car and right after I signed the title, it slid off the roof. It slid perfectly over the stainless trim on the rain gutter, down the glass of the driver's door, and, hovering flat against the glass, it slid right between the glass and the window felt. It had to slide perfectly to land itself inside the door – totally inaccessible. You can use a coat hanger to get a door unlocked, but not to pull a title up out of a door. I think it was God asking me if I was really sure. I had to get some tools and take the door panel off to get the title out for Scott.

We tithed the sale, used some of the money to pay debt, and used the rest to cash flow our upcoming wedding.

Red, the Corvette was a different story. This was a specialized car used for racing that occurs two or three times a year. It had an automatic transmission, not a manual transmission, so it wasn't a track car. I had a friend who open-road raced with me and had a fabrication shop try to help me sell it for a while. After that failed, I sold it to my brother for a dollar for him to sell. He finally did get a buyer and netted himself enough money to put a good set of pipes on his Harley Davidson motor cycle. That car would be called stupid tax. I easily had over $20,000 in the car. The motor was hardly broken in, with just a few dozen autocross passes on it – just enough to realize I was sheering the oil because of the tightness of the engine and to resolve the problem with a big oil cooler.

God's Timing and Provision

Susan and I dated for a year before our engagement. I tried proposing on day 364, she returned the ring. The next day was a year and she accepted the proposal. We had a fifteen month long engagement prior to our wedding.

I had been working for the startup Alacritech for just over six years at the time of our wedding. Shortly before the wedding, I needed to write a job description for a position I needed to fill. I started by looking on some of the job posting sites for similar roles to help me write the advertisement. As I was doing this research, I found a job posting for a job that was basically what I was doing at the time for Alacritech. This role was at a public company, and at a senior director level rather than the director level I had held the previous six years. In my eyes I was the perfect candidate for the job. I applied, and I also found a friend through LinkedIn that had contacts at the company and used him to do a back-door referral for the position. I waited weeks and didn't hear anything. I got pretty frustrated during that time. I couldn't understand why I wasn't even getting screened.

Susan had a small business. Tax preparation was a challenge for her. Here it was August and she hadn't met with her accountant yet to prepare the previous year's return, now four months late. I went with her to the appointment. Shortly after we returned to her apartment that afternoon, I received a phone call from the recruiter. Within a week or two I had a half-day interview with the company. After the interview, the hiring manager said he had other candidates he was interviewing and would get back to me within a few days. Later that afternoon, I had a job offer with a salary that pretty much equaled my old salary and Susan's business income, with bonuses and stock options on top of the base compensation. I started the new job seven weeks before our wedding, having negotiated a long weekend for the wedding and extended paid time off over Christmas for the surprise honeymoon I was planning.

The new job was evidence of grace, replacing Susan's business income since it wasn't practical to commute one to two hours to clean houses. Despite that grace, Susan had grave concerns about the travel requirements. She was concerned the travel would be a challenge for my younger son, Alexander, and his need for consistency with his autism. God had a different plan, because the travel ended up being one of the biggest initial blessings of the position.

For our honeymoon I planned a few days in St. Thomas, US Virgin Islands, followed by a week-long cruise on the WindStar Wind Spirit, a 150-passenger motorized sailing yacht. My parents stayed with Jonathan and Alexander (then 17 and 16) during the honeymoon. Alexander, who was struggling with the marriage, chose not to attend the wedding, even though he attended his mother's wedding the month before. He was attending a special needs school in Alameda at the time, struggling again in school.

Shortly after the honeymoon, Alexander had issues and we had to get police and mental health assistance. This wasn't the first time we had needed police assistance but the first time we had to put him under an involuntary mental health hold. At the end of the three days, Susan and I went to the hospital to pick him up. We barely got on the freeway after his discharge when he threatened grave bodily harm. I pulled off at the next exit and returned to the hospital for another involuntary hold.

Several years earlier, I had struggled to get his education needs met in the public school. After reading an article about a local special education advocate, I retained this lawyer to litigate against the school system to allow Alexander to get his needs met. US Education Law under the Individuals with Disabilities Act ensures those with special needs get an educational placement appropriate for their needs. At the lawyer's recommendation, we had Alexander assessed by a psychologist and received a solid diagnosis of Asperger's Syndrome. Following the diagnosis, the lawyer negotiated with the school system for a placement at a private school specializing with Asperger's and similar conditions.

During the second involuntary hold, one of the psychologists caring for Alexander quickly assessed school placement being a key component affecting his stability. His recommendation was to go to the press and hire a lawyer to sue the school system. While I considered going to the press, I did retain the special needs attorney again, and we had an emergency hearing while Alexander was still in the hospital. From that hearing, the school system agreed to a placement at a special program in Michigan. Within days, Alexander, his mother, and I were flying to Michigan to enroll him at the school.

Three months after I took this new job where we thought the travel was going to be detrimental to Alexander, it became a blessing. Over the next year and a half, while he was at the Michigan school and a subsequent school in Iowa prior to his 18th birthday, I was given the blessing of business travel that allowed me to visit him every three or four weeks by just scheduling long layovers in Chicago, Detroit, or Minneapolis.

I know Alexander still has anger from some of the parenting choices I made with him. Some of this was particularly challenging during the periods where I was single-parenting while his mom was struggling with her disease. I did the best I could with the tools I had at the time, just as my parents did the best they could with the tools they had.

I'm grateful today to have a restored relationship with my parents and relationships with both my sons, as Susan has with her biological sons. We do the best we can as stepparents to each of our respective stepsons. We pray that all the boys will eventually have relationships with both their parents.

> *An excellent wife who can find?*
> *She is far more precious than jewels.*[7]

---

[7] Proverbs 31:10

You have captivated my heart, my sister, my bride;
  you have captivated my heart with one glance of your eyes,
  with one jewel of your necklace.[8]

Then the Lord God said, "It is not good that the man should be
alone; I will make him a helper fit for him."[9]

I am a blessed man. Susan is an essential part of who I am today, and she provides priceless support for the ministry. We had to grow quickly as new believers in Christ in the early days of our relationship. Through repentance, humility, and obedience, God prepared us for the roles He has us in today.

---

[8] Song of Solomon 4:9
[9] Genesis 2:18

Chapter Three – Missions

Susan asked the fateful question, "Would you ever want to do missions work?" as we were getting married. In our second year of marriage, we joined our church on a short-term trip to Paraguay to do some construction and evangelism work. This trip was the first one our church had made to support long-term missionaries the church had sent to Paraguay 18 years earlier. While the trip was eye-opening into the reality of the missions field, including the spiritual warfare of the work, it was clear that my calling wasn't evangelism.

We started a cadence of trips every two years. Our second trip was to Kenya, Africa. The prior year, through God's providence, we had moved to Huntington Beach. Alexander had finished school, and we had to then sell the house to close out the property separation from the divorce. In a down market in 2009, God brought us 23 offers, and one of the cash buyers closed in 17 days from listing the house.

When we moved to Huntington Beach, we started church shopping and felt very welcome at the Evangelical Free Church of Huntington Beach, now Beach Bible Church. The church had a long association with Bible translation, sharing the parking lot with Wycliffe Bible Translators for several decades when Wycliffe Bible Translators was headquartered in California.

Our first mission trip with the Evangelical Free Church of Huntington Beach was to run a Vacation Bible School for the missionary kids of the Uganda-Tanzania branch of the Summer Institute of Linguistics. Missionaries from Wycliffe Bible Translators serving overseas are typically seconded[10] to the Summer Institute of Linguistics. While it

---

[10]A secondment arrangement involves an employee being temporarily assigned to a different employer altogether

29

was good serving the kids, I remember thinking that the linguists were strange, and I could never see myself as a Bible translator. Little did I know what God had in store.

While being a Bible translator was off my bucket list, we were very involved in missions at the Evangelical Free Church of Huntington Beach. We both served on the missions committee, and I chaired the committee for a period. The missions fund supported about two dozen families, including about a dozen mission families with Wycliffe Bible Translators.

In 2012 we were on a family vacation to Sanibel, Florida, for a family reunion. My brothers went to Disney World for a day. We took a trip to the Wycliffe Bible Translators headquarters and the Discovery Center to visit some of the families the church was supporting.

Ironically, at that point we were not in strong relationship with Wycliffe Associates, who are on the same campus as Wycliffe Bible Translators, so we did not visit Wycliffe Associates during this trip.

Chicken Dinners

One of the activities of Wycliffe Associates is the Wycliffe Associates Banquet. This is a series of lunch or dinner events, where typically a chicken dinner is served and a presentation is made about Bible translation. Currently, Wycliffe Associates hosts about 300 banquets a year as part of the marketing program. The banquets make a financial contribution to the work but also serve as an awareness tool to attract volunteers and staff.

One of our friends on the missions board, a retired Wycliffe Bible Translators missionary in her early 80s at the time, invited us to go to the Spring 2010 Wycliffe Associates Banquet in Newport Beach. At the banquet we learned about faith promises and made our first of what we thought was significant at the time faith promise for missions. Wycliffe Associates resonated much more strongly to Susan and me –

their mission was to advance Bible translation, but they did it through activities that were more in areas Susan and I were gifted.

In 2011 we were invited to the Wycliffe Associates President's Summit in Southern California. Being local, it seemed like a nice, inexpensive weekend getaway at an area luxury beachfront hotel. Little did we know how much this weekend would change our lives.

Over the next several years, that initial free chicken dinner that had set the hook saw us being reeled deeper and deeper into a life of transformation.

Never and All In

In the fall of 2012, Susan and I went back to Vermont to visit her mother, siblings, and extended family. I remember asking Susan if she had any desire to move back home – perhaps operate a bed and breakfast inn (AirBnB didn't exist yet). She quickly responded, "No, never." Susan is a beach girl, loves the ocean, and we were living five minutes from the beach in Huntington Beach, drawing a huge salary, and enjoying life.

Fast forward five months. Susan's then 84-year-old mother took a fall in the doctor's office and broke her back. After we got word, we made plans to return to Vermont because Susan's mom needed extended care for the injury.

My boss at the time was commuting to work in Southern California from Oregon, and another executive was commuting from Seattle. We had operations in Massachusetts, Northern California, Southern California, and India. Most of my work involved teleconferences, because we had a global operation. We also spent a fair amount of time with customers and suppliers in Texas, North Carolina, and China.

A day or two after the meeting, I was working in the kitchen, and Susan came up and said, "I think I need to stay for a while," to which I responded, "yes, like three years." God had been working on both of our hearts that it was time to practice what 2 Timothy teaches and take care of the widow. We had Susan's mom Gladys out for extended winter visits, but this was different.

When we arrived in Vermont, the hospital social worker conducted a family meeting to discuss her mom's care. Susan, most of her siblings, and I attended. It was clear Gladys was going to need live-in care.

So, with six siblings in the immediate area, we found ourselves moving in with Gladys to provide her care. We took one day at a time, not knowing if it would be a 3-month or 3-year commitment.

In the fall of 2014, we attended the WA President's Summit, an annual tradition for us by that point. We were asked to give a short testimony about our support for Bible translation. I don't remember everything Susan and I said, but I do recall saying we were "all in." Little did we know how much God could stretch all in. Shortly before the conference, our Area Director, Bill McDonald, asked if we were interested in a vision trip to India. With a number of coworkers either living in India or immigrated to the US from India, it wasn't a hard sell. There was also this exciting new thing called MAST that we would be able to see.

MAST

At the summit we heard of this new thing that Wycliffe Associates was testing called MAST (Mobilized Assistance Supporting Translation). Up to this point, Wycliffe Associates was only indirectly supporting Bible translation with construction programs, aircraft purchases, satellite terminal installations, and supplying support staff to assist Bible translation efforts. They did have a successful English Language Learning program to help national translators learn English so they could better interact with their translation consultants and could access English language translation resources.

Chapter Three

During the vision trip to India in March of 2015, we saw several paradigms of Bible translation. We visited the Institute of Language and Linguistics in Dehradun and learned how they equip national translators. We visited Operation Agape, a discipleship and church planting organization, and saw how they were doing Bible translation with artificial intelligence-based software. Finally, we were able to participate as facilitators in a MAST event outside of Bangalore. This was one of the first few MAST events ever held and was the first one where outsiders participated.

Prior to this trip, I had read Bob Creson's book *The Finish Line* (Creson, 2014), a call to action to partner with Wycliffe Bible Translators to finish the task of Bible translation. I was troubled by two aspects of the book. First, it seemed to be a call to the starting line, where translation was started in the last language rather than the call to the finish line. Also, as far as the finish line, it was not clear when or if these languages would have complete Bibles.

In addition to falling in love with the simple elegance of MAST, where the local Body of Christ was equipped and empowered to do their own Bible translation, I was introduced to the Gateway Language Strategy and open licensing through Creative Commons.

As I worked with national Bible translators in this first workshop, I saw two major barriers to greater participation by national translators related to copyright and source material. Typically, when a translation was done, the church didn't own the Bible, the Bible Society did, so the church was beholden to the Bible Society and their capacity and willingness to do reprints or make revisions or different editions. So often we see Bibles that are decades old badly in need of revision, and the church is unable to get a revision or even a reprint of the existing edition. Secondly, most translation resources are in English, since modern Bible translation evolved from sending western missionaries to the world.

The use of open licensing, under the Creative Commons ensured the church retained control of the translation by preventing anyone from closing the translation. The church would then be free to make derivatives, such as audio Bibles or study Bibles, and would be able to make revisions to their Bible.

On the resource side, Wycliffe Associates had an initiative, the Gateway Language Program, to translate an openly licensed Bible, and a series of helps, including comprehension questions, translation notes to explain difficult passages, and a translation dictionary with important terms, definitions, and where the terms are used throughout the Bible.

It was clear that MAST changed everything. I was so convicted that I wrote a Call to Action to Bob Creson, whom I had not yet met. As the former missions chair from the Evangelical Free Church of Huntington Beach, where the church supported his late Chief Operating Officer (before Forest's untimely death) and a number of other Wycliffe Bible Translators headquarters staff and field staff, I felt I had the right to send the note. Whether Bob received it and acted upon it was a different issue. I did receive some pushback from some of my friends from the Evangelical Free Church of Huntington Beach who were closer to Wycliffe Bible Translators. On the other hand, Bruce Smith, whom I copied on the email was encouraged by it. In the email I expressed partnership opportunities I saw with Wycliffe Associates to complete the task of Bible translation by the year 2025. At the time I didn't fully understand how difficult it would be to partner with traditional Bible translation organization nor how different were our respective missions.

Sabbatical

Clearly, the MAST trip enlightened us. We were so excited, we signed up to come back for a follow-up event in September where the groups were expected to complete the translation of the fifty Open Bible Stories they were translating. The Coordinator for South Asia wanted us for two weeks, but I didn't feel I could take that much vacation.

Well, upon arrival at home, we found that the company I had been working at for the previous nine years was under a tender offer to be acquired by a Singaporean company. During the acquisition, my boss was strongly suggesting that if I didn't move back to Southern California, I was at a high risk to not have a job following the close of the transaction. I offered to commute at my own expense and have an apartment, but Susan's mom's care was a higher priority than keeping the California job.

In early May the transaction closed, and the following day I was notified of my termination. The company would have me consult for three months; then if I signed a release, I would have a severance package.

I emailed Dan Kramer after this and said I have good news – I got fired and Susan and I could go to India for both weeks, not just one. Dan replied back, "It's a little strange to say 'that's great' when it involves job elimination, but their loss could be our gain." Nearly four years later I haven't asked him if it was Wycliffe Associates' gain – but I haven't had to either.

Susan and I discussed what I wanted to do for the next season of life. I had been helping a friend build a large, timber-framed barn and had a desire to build my own. I also had opportunities to do more technology consulting. Finally, MAST was intriguing. Ultimately, we decided I would take a one-year sabbatical starting in August when my employment ended and decide what I wanted to do when I grew up. In God's providence, through this transition Susan and I had peace beyond understanding, despite the loss of ongoing secular employment with a very significant compensation package.

Ultimately over the next year, I did multiple trips to India, a trip to West Africa, and a trip to Thailand to facilitate MAST. In January 2016, Dan asked me to look for opportunities in all the regions and we'd be able to see where I might fit in the organization. By August, when I returned from Thailand, I had either served in the region or served with the leadership of every region of the world where Wycliffe Associates operates except the Pacific.

Upon returning on August 6th, I had a text message from Dan: "Hi Joe (and welcome back), I'm not sure what time zone you're in, but would it be possible to connect sometime later this evening or tomorrow? I'd like to catch up and also share an idea with you (yes, run…) :-)."

I'd been warned in the past about the danger of rides in Dan's car or other one-on-one situations where Dan would provide opportunities too good to pass up.

Dan and I talked over the weekend and he asked me to consider taking on the Gateway Language Director Role for the Pacific. Susan and I recognized I was having a lot more satisfaction working with MAST than I was in high technology, even though the income was vastly different.

The following month, I attended my first meeting as a member of the Wycliffe Associates Board of Trustees. In my introduction, Bruce made the comment that I'm the only person he knows where working with over 100 languages with MAST is considered a sabbatical.

Mansion with Many Rooms

Every time we go on a mission trip, leaving for home is always the hardest part. You make friends during these trips, and even though you know they will be with you for eternity after we leave this earth, there's the pain in your heart of saying goodbye and not knowing if you will see them again this side of heaven.

After years of this pain, I finally got a great word picture of this pain. In John Jesus talks of his Father's house having many rooms.[11] What I finally saw was the Holy Spirit renovating my heart to add on a few more rooms for all my new brothers and sisters in Christ.

A Strong Marriage

As the mission activity picked up with Wycliffe Associates, it was clear Susan and I were in a season of different mission callings. She was caring for her mother full time, and I was being called to the South Pacific and South Asia to serve the Bibleless people of the world. Susan is as invested in the Bible translation ministry as I am, God just has her participating from Vermont.

With this, I felt a calling to have a stronger marriage. Discussing this with Susan was a big challenge. What I wanted to convey was "I want the best marriage possible." What she heard was "Our marriage is in trouble."

Our marriage has been great since the beginning. Being a second marriage for both of us, after a failed marriage each, second marriages are a risk. It was clear from the beginning that God was at and needed to stay at the center of this marriage. If we kept Him first, then we'd have a strong marriage. Our wedding rings are a reminder of this – a cord of three.

> *And though a man might prevail against one who is alone, two will withstand him—a threefold cord is not quickly broken.*[12]

In a season where I was travelling significantly – in 2018 I was away from home over 80% of the time and away from Susan over 70% of the time – travel can place significant stress on marriage. Thanks to technology today, we can still have quality time when I'm half a world

---

[11] John 14:2
[12] Ecclesiastes 4:12

away. Little did I know the impact of this when I saw the first Internet telephony demonstration at an Interop conference in the early 1990s. In many locations, I can do video calls, and if the time zone allows, I'll do that morning and night. With Internet telephony and videoconferencing tools, it costs pennies a day to maintain this critical link and share our days while we are apart.

While I don't recall us doing anything specific to improve our marriage, what we did do is commit to no compromises but the best for the marriage. It has been challenging, because Susan's first marriage covenant was broken by infidelity multiple times. With my role involving working with men and women, Satan certainly attempted to leverage that past wound to create doubt, when there was nothing to doubt. This resulted in me ensuring that Susan also develops relationships with the women I serve with in ministry. I also must ensure that I never allow a situation on which Satan can capitalize.

Weeping with Jesus

We're getting to the end of Susan's season as a caregiver for her mother. One early morning I found Susan out in our war room praying and worshiping God as she was working through accepting that it is time to consider palliative care for her mother.

I joined her, and eventually we embraced and danced to the worship music. As we were dancing, I had this strong visual of Jesus walking over to us, His arms outstretched for a group hug. As that vision crystalized, I just lost it and started weeping in the Spirit at how much Jesus loves us. The only problem – my mouth was mere inches, if that, from Susan's ear and she jumped away and said, "That was my ear you just wept in!"

I recently read a book on intercessory prayer by Cindy Jacobs (Jacobs, 2018). In it she talks about manifestations of intercession such as weeping and laughing. She also says that sometimes these strong emotions can take the intercessor quite by surprise – I can personally attest to that, as can those who have experienced when this manifests through me.

Ministry Together

My heart's desire is for Susan to serve by my side. I travel to many beautiful island nations and work with wonderful brothers and sisters in Christ, but Susan only gets to live vicariously through my stories. We're expecting that in 2020 Susan's mom will be home with Jesus and Susan will be able to serve alongside me.

In the summer of 2018, God showed me that Susan will be with me. I got this clear vision of us attending a dedication for the 100th MAST translation in Papua New Guinea. It was a sweet, sweet vision, and one I can't wait to see fulfilled.

Even though we are in different locations much of the time, the Wycliffe Associates work is only possible with Susan's encouragement and support. She gives me desperately needed perspective and is always praying for me and the team. This isn't surprising. Even with Jesus' ministry, there were women like Mary and Martha behind Jesus and the disciples providing support. God gave me the counterpart I need to serve His Kingdom.

> *Husbands, love your wives, as Christ loved the church and gave himself up for her*[13]

---

[13] Ephesisans 5:25

Section Two

For consider your calling, brothers: not many of you were wise according to worldly standards, not many were powerful, not many were of noble birth. But God chose what is foolish in the world to shame the wise; God chose what is weak in the world to shame the strong. [14]

The stone that the builders rejected
  has become the cornerstone.
This is the Lord's doing;
  it is marvelous in our eyes.[15]

---

[14] 1 Corinthians 1:26-27
[15] Psalm 118:22-23

Chapter Four – No Conflict in Ministry – Right?

In the summer of 2018, I was partnered with a new Regional Director. He was a former CEO of a partner Bible translation organization and then came to serve with Wycliffe Associates. I met him in 2017 when he was a guest speaker at our annual President's Summit events.

In our first joint trip we were to visit our staff in Papua New Guinea. The trip did not start well for me. With a series of domestic travel disruptions, I arrived two days late to Papua New Guinea. I was to fly on Monday from Albany, New York, to Los Angeles via Charlotte and continue on to Papua New Guinea via Brisbane, Australia. Well, there was inclement weather on Monday and flights were late into Charlotte. It turns out the connecting flight was delayed waiting on the crew. When the flight crew arrived, we began boarding. Shortly after I sat down, they halted the boarding process. It turns out one of the flight attendants was going to hit her Federal Aviation Administration work limit for the day during the flight, so wasn't eligible to fly. The crew worked with operations to get another flight attendant, but all the standby attendants at the airport had been assigned. They then had to call in an attendant, which has a two-hour reporting window. By the time the attendant arrived, others on the crew timed out, and I found myself sleeping on the floor in Charlotte since hotel rooms were sold out.

I had to gamble the next day on whether to connect through Washington DC, where there were many flights, or Austin, Texas, where there was only one flight through to Los Angeles. I took the DC option and faced an aircraft that needed its tail greased. By the time we arrived in Los Angeles, the Qantas connection had departed, one of the few nights I've been in Los Angeles and the flight to Brisbane wasn't delayed. Many nights the New York to Los Angeles flight arrives late, delaying the Brisbane flight. The fifth day I finally got to Australia and on to Papua New Guinea, giving me only one day there while my counterpart arrived two days earlier. We then traveled together to Singapore and he was getting ill with heart spasms. I have a strong group of prayer supporters, so I put out an update in my confidential prayer letter and asked for prayer for him. This created a learning opportunity for me that has taken me over a year to fully comprehend, realizing some big clues on the cultural misstep I took. The feedback I received at the time is that I should have consulted him before putting personal information about him in my prayer newsletter.

The Conflict

Over the next eleven months things between the two of us would vacillate between good, okay, bad, and very bad. We never worked well as a team. Our leadership styles were very different. I thought I was following the servant leadership model that the Wycliffe Associates senior leadership model so well, and I surmised he was using his CEO and Asian Dean leadership model, which a North American finds very different. My frustration rippled down into my team and the difference in styles was visible in the respective teams. Certainly, conflict in the field team happened alongside the conflict between us.

Madang

In February of 2019, I attended a MAST event in Madang, Papua New Guinea. At the event I was given an offer I couldn't refuse. Two local church leaders, Koil and Kautum, approached me and said, "We're tired of waiting, can you help us reach all the languages of Madang this year?" My first question – how many languages? Their response: 200-300. When it is obvious God is moving, you want to align your ministry with God. I remember reading in *The Insanity of God* (Ripken & Lewis, 2012) about Nik's struggles in getting meetings in Asia when God was calling him to Central Asia. Over the course of about two months a doctor was trying to get him to travel to a central Asia country, and Nik refused multiple invitations. At the same time, he was having his scheduled itinerary interrupted by events like the 18 pastors he was meeting being jailed ahead of the meeting, the next group being hospitalized after a car accident, and other disruptions to planned meetings. In the end he found the Holy Spirit had been trying, through this doctor, to get him to disciple five new Muslim background believers. You need to be where God is working and where God wants you.

I told the two men that Wycliffe Associates couldn't possibly do that this year; but if they could raise up 25 leaders, we would teach them to equip the language groups themselves. By the next morning Kautum handed me a list of 23 names, several of them facilitating at the current event. Through God's providence, I had a team coming to Papua in late March to train a similar group of church leaders. That same team was able to travel across the border to Madang to train this group the first week of April – a mere six weeks after this event. In the third week of April I was back in Madang, and another large MAST event was being held. These newly trained leaders were providing the primary leadership at the training.

Bulldozer

The intent with this team wasn't to merely facilitate large events, just as Wycliffe Associates was, but to actually go into the villages and conduct the training there. This significantly changes the economics of training language groups, since it costs far less to move a facilitator into a village and have the village host the facilitator and the village's translation team, than to bring the translators and facilitators to a central location for the training. It also strengthens the local ownership of the project, since the entire village has the opportunity to participate right from inception of the project.

With the desire of the Madang church to get 200 translations done this year, I was getting increasingly frustrated at the pace of language vetting. Once we get a request from a church or language group for training, we validate if there are other translation projects for the language and what code should be assigned to the project for language identification. Koil had supplied a large number of languages for this vetting process to our field operations team immediately after the February event. We were now entering May, and the vetting of most of them wasn't finished and language codes weren't identified or assigned.

Susan has a term of endearment for me. It is "bulldozer." Sometimes (perhaps frequently), I plow forward without looking at what may be in my path. With my mounting frustration on the delays to deploying this team due to the vetting, I was getting more and more vocal with Dan. At the same time, Dan was getting pressure from his leadership about language start pace. With this confluence, Dan talked to Brent Ropp as they were settling in for a flight. As they settled in, Dan was running two text conversations – one back and forth with Brent and a second with me. From the conversations, I received a green light to finish the vetting of the languages for this team. In true bulldozer mode, I plowed right over my field operations counterpart, and moved forward with getting the job done. Languages were waiting and we were in the way.

Surrender

My carnage resulted in an email response from my counterpart questioning my character, since he had not received any heads up from his leadership on the change. I had gotten up in the middle of the night and made the mistake of reading email when I got up. The response spun me up, so when I couldn't get back to sleep, I went out to my war room. During my sabbatical, I restored a ~250-year-old timber frame building and put it up as a two-story barn/garage/workshop. While I was building it, I had many of the original studs, which were 3″ x 3″ pieces of oak, with a nice patina and lots of nail holes. As I was working on the barn one day, God told me to make a cross from some of this oak, so I made a six-foot-high cross and hung it on the north wall of the second-floor woodworking studio. Susan and I have spent many hours individually and collectively praying for Bible translation in that room.

In the war room I got prostrate and started praying. After a while, I got up to read some scripture on my phone in the corner. Following the scripture reading, I started walking back to the prayer rug. On the wall around the cross, I've been hanging travel gifts as prayer reminders for the people I serve. I touched a bilum (string bag) I received in Madang, Papua New Guinea, in April. At that event, we had a translator that fell down during morning worship. We thought she might have been sick or injured, but the Holy Spirit had her in a fetal position. A short time later she started speaking out for Madang to repent, the Matapi tribe to repent, the Gal tribe to repent. In the last 15 years there was a cult run by the Black Jesus[16] in Matapi and Gal. There were thousands of followers, and there were very evil practices - including rape, human sacrifices, drinking of human blood, and cannibalism. At the end of the event, this translator gave me the bilum.

When I touched the bag, the Holy Spirit immediately had me down prostrate and weeping in the Spirit. This is one gifting that I am learning to accept. More and more frequently, the Spirit has me weeping as the Spirit is grieved. This was one case – the focus shouldn't have been my peer or me – the focus needs to be the Bibleless people that need God's Word to help disciple them and bring them to repentance. The timing on this was amazing. In my normal Bible reading plan, I was in Revelation 5 that morning. While my weeping wasn't over nobody being able to open the scroll, it was pretty close to

---

[16] https://en.wikipedia.org/wiki/Steven_Tari

the context of verse 4, being on all the Bibleless people that don't even have a scroll to read. I read on and got to verses 9-10 – this is what I live for – to get scripture to every tribe, language, people, and nation. It just cemented my sin in this conflict: taking my eyes off Jesus and the calling God had for me.

Publicly Chastise

Things weren't resolved after my prayer time. They escalated a bit more and we had a face-to-face meeting with our supervisors and our Vice President. Resolution didn't come out of that meeting; but a couple days later, the two of us were having a private meeting reviewing a presentation we were giving to the rest of the operations team. I had put a comment in there that there was conflict within the region's leadership, and we were working through it. My peer got very upset with me and asked if I was trying to publicly chastise him. I shared how when I point a finger at him, there are three fingers pointing at me. By saying the leadership is working through some conflict, it wasn't assigning blame, it was acknowledging our situation.

> *"Truly, I say to you, whatever you bind on earth shall be bound in heaven, and whatever you loose on earth shall be loosed in heaven. Again I say to you, if two of you agree on earth about anything they ask, it will be done for them by my Father in heaven. For where two or three are gathered in my name, there am I among them."*[17]

God intervened between us in that room. The Holy Spirit worked in both of us and supernatural healing took place. This is a conflict that lasted for months and wasn't resolved with months of mediation by our senior leadership. Yet in mere minutes the Holy Spirit gave us mutual understanding and deep spiritual harmony that could only

---

[17] Matthew 18:18-20

come from God. We were able to pray for each other, put it all behind us, and have a revitalized working relationship.

Sweet Harmony

We had sweet harmony following this and were really starting to work together as a team. Within weeks we got word that a major restructuring was taking place and the roles were being merged. I feel some regret that after all these months of strife, as soon as it was resolved we change how we work together within the new organization structure. On the other hand, I am grateful for the time in the refiner's fire, praying for the fruit of longsuffering, and know both of us are a better fit for the Kingdom because of the trial.

> *Beloved, do not be surprised at the fiery trial when it comes upon you to test you, as though something strange were happening to you. But rejoice insofar as you share Christ's sufferings, that you may also rejoice and be glad when his glory is revealed.*[18]

> *Moab has been at ease from his youth and has settled on his dregs; he has not been emptied from vessel to vessel, nor has he gone into exile; so his taste remains in him, and his scent is not changed. "Therefore, behold, the days are coming declares the Lord, when I shall send to him pourers who will pour him, and empty his vessels and break his jars in pieces.*[19]

---

[18] 1 Peter 4:12-13
[19] Jeremiah 48:11-12

Chapter Five – Indonesian Gateway Language
Maria

One of my early staff members in Indonesia was Maria. I met her at the first Bahasa Indonesia Gateway Language event in the fall of 2016. She quickly exhibited leadership and organizational skills necessary to be a team leader for this project.

I spoke to Maria about her calling, and she did not have a specific word direct from God or prophetic word that confirmed her participation in the ministry. She did have people say confirming things, including random people saying something that just struck to the heart.

Her commitment to the ministry came from values her father instilled in her and her two brothers, an ethic that one must contribute to your God and to your country.

Early on in my participation with MAST, I would be at events and would be called Pastor Joe. I have no formal seminary training and have not been ordained by man. In the beginning it bothered me, and I would correct the pastors and others that referred to me as pastor and say I am not a pastor. As I understood scripture better, today I realize that in God's kingdom, we are all kings and priests[20].

Recently, I was reading the book *A Passion for God: The Spiritual Journey of A. W. Tozer* (Dorsett, 2008), and came across the prayer he said to God upon his ordination in 1919. This is a man that would rise to the top leadership of the Christian and Missionary Alliance, yet had no formal Bible school training. God does that on occasion. My friend John from Australia rose to be president of the Baptist denomination in Queensland, Australia, again with no formal Bible school training. I

---

[20] 1 Peter 2:9, Revelation 5:10

shared Tozer's prayer with Susan, and we both saw how that prayer applied so well to my anointing by God – it reflects the words that I should have used, though I would have used modern English, not King James English. Tozer's "Prayer of a Minor Prophet" is included in Appendix One.

Maria was one of the early disciples on the team that really helped me understand that my role was a small part leader, a bigger part pastor and shepherd. We faced lots of intense spiritual warfare through this project. Some of that was at events, some of it was direct attacks on staff and family, including Maria and her family.

Heartbreak

During the period we worked together on the Gateway Language project, Maria had a growing family, with two young daughters. She also had a husband that struggled with her travels with the ministry. This greatly strained the marriage. The strain on the marriage was heartbreaking for Maria. She also was committed to seeing the Bible in every language in Indonesia.

We spent many hours talking about the challenges and praying. Maria lost her dad when she was a young college student and over time, she came to feel that God brought us together to give her a second earthly father. Certainly, she was maturing her relationship with her heavenly Father, but she also wanted someone to talk to here.

As a ministry worker, extra care must be taken when working with members of the opposite sex. I've had colleagues fall and subsequently leave the ministry. With the spiritual warfare we face, I had to be hypervigilant to ensure that even the perception of impropriety couldn't take place.

The sweet part of this is through the discipling of Maria, she was able to take on the same role with her staff. Our later conversations transitioned from personal discipling of Maria to leading and coaching her in her discipling and shepherding of her staff.

Junkies

One of the events Maria led was the event we started on the Papuan Malay New Testament. It was a challenging event. We were using a new tool, V-MAST, and it had never been used at this scale. We spent the first two days fighting server and network issues.

We also had staffing challenges. We had invited over a dozen pastors and thirty students from the local Christian university. Only a small number of the invited students arrived, so we had to expand the recruiting. We had students invite their Papuan Malay speaking friends from the university.

Some of these students weren't the typical students that would be recruited for this project. In fact, Maria was mortified as they started showing up. I remember one that had a jacket with profanity on it. These students referred to themselves as the Junkies. They had the reputation of the drinkers on campus. Yet these were the students God chose to make history.

God did two amazing things at this event. First, despite the technology issues, the entire New Testament was translated and thoroughly checked in five and a half days. This was the first translation we're aware of that was completed in less than a week. The more important thing we witnessed was the transformation of the Junkies.

I also learned about obedience to the Spirit. I had been reading Nik Ripken's *Insanity of God* (Ripken & Lewis, 2012), and he talks about being called to disciple some Muslim background believers. In getting to know these men, he heard their testimonies about how they came to acquire their Bibles – the miracles of the Holy Spirit in getting Bibles to these men in creative ways. I had to speak a word of encouragement to the translators and wanted to share that story. As I walked to the podium I redirected and talked about Acts chapter 8, and the question of how the Ethiopian got that scroll of Isaiah.

The fascinating part of this is that the next morning, Pastor Yan delivered his devotion, and he picked up where I left off in Acts chapter 8 – talking about Peter's obedience and how we have to go where called to evangelize. Same story – we each approached it from the opposite perspective. I talked to Pastor Yan later in the week and asked when he prepared that message. He had prepared that message a full two months earlier, yet the Holy Spirit had me doing the introductory part just mere hours earlier, solely relying on my obedience to His prompting.

We had a closing ceremony on the last day and the pastors prayed for all the students. We then heard the testimony of a number of the Junkies. The story was similar – loss of one or both parents at a young age, anger at God for the loss – separation from God. At the workshop, the time in the Word helped them see God's love for them that began a healing process in them and drew them back to God. The Holy Spirit can work an amazing transformation when someone spends six to eight hours a day for two solid weeks dwelling in scripture.

It reminds me a lot of the parable of the lost sheep in Luke 15. We're saying these sinners shouldn't be here at the table, but these are exactly who Jesus wants to minister to. We see this time and time again at events hosted by Wycliffe Associates and our MAST partners. God draws who He wants to the events and then we see miraculous transformation.

Betrayal

During all this time, Maria was working with a partner organization. There was an issue in the office and Maria was a whistleblower. Unfortunately, Indonesian labor practice doesn't provide the same protection for whistleblowers as US law, and it became a very difficult situation for Maria so she had to leave the organization. It was also becoming clear that Wycliffe Associates had to discontinue their partnership with that organization.

Maria is still sad today that these close friends, her brothers and sisters in Christ, have abandoned her and more importantly appear to have abandoned the Lord today.

We moved the continuation of the Gateway Language work to Bahasa Technology Solutions (BTS), and Maria joined BTS. A short time later, we held another event. At this event a letter was sent by the former partner to the university discrediting the work to disrupt the event. While this seemed like just a human conflict, it was a replay of a spiritual attack we had seen in Papua New Guinea about six months prior. The attack targeted the students, who were less sure of their faith, rather than the pastors.

> *Anyone whom you forgive, I also forgive. Indeed, what I have forgiven, if I have forgiven anything, has been for your sake in the presence of Christ, so that we would not be outwitted by Satan; for we are not ignorant of his designs.*[21]

Sawi

The Sawi are the people that Don Richardson ministered to in Irian Jaya, now Papua, Indonesia, the people of Peace Child fame. Don and his wife Carol lived with this stone-age tribe from the early sixties through the mid-seventies. Don later was an ambassador for missions, speaking at 40 conferences a year. For years he supported Wycliffe Associates, speaking at our banquets and President's Summits. Susan and I met Don at a President's Summit in 2012, and I recall having breakfast with him one morning during that summit.

---

[21] 2 Corinthians 2:10-11

In June of 2018, as Don was dying of brain cancer, Bruce Smith and Brent Ropp attended an event where Don received a lifetime achievement award for his work in missions and as a missions ambassador. Bruce, Brent, and Don's son Steve, president of Pioneers, felt the plaque Don received wasn't commensurate with his achievements, so there was discussion on how Don could be better honored. Don started translating the Sawi New Testament in the 1960s, finishing it in the early 1970s, and it has been available to the Sawi since the 1990s; but the Old Testament was never completed. It was decided that the best way to honor Don would be to equip the Sawi to complete the work he had started half a century earlier.

Yanti did some survey work to find the Sawi people. Bruce covers her search for the Sawi in his book *Living Translation, Peace Children – The Sawi Story* (Smith, 2020). Yanti is profiled a few chapters later in *Pacific Saints* as I cover the Papua Team. Following engagement with the Sawi, the Indonesian MAST team was engaged to lead a MAST event for their Old Testament. This was to be the largest single language MAST event, though coming in to the event, it sounded like at least two Sawi dialects[22] would participate.

I received some questions from the Wycliffe Associates leadership team about not having any expats leading the event, but I'd been coaching Maria for the past three years as she led our Gateway Language program for Bahasa Indonesian. She had participated in a few MAST events and led many Gateway language events. At the Gateway language events, she and her team orchestrated a language team to

---

[22] The definitions of the terms "language" and "dialect" may overlap and are often subject to debate, with the differentiation between the two classifications often grounded in arbitrary and/or sociopolitical motives. From the perspective of the native speaker of a dialect, it is always considered a language – their language, even if there is similarity with a neighboring language.

translate hundreds of chapters of scripture or supporting helps in a single event. A single-language or two-language event for the Old Testament was something she was well prepared to co-lead. She was teamed up with Sierra, who had led numerous events with 100-200 translators, albeit working in groups of 10 per language on the same content. Between the two of them, they had all the core skills and experience to lead the event. I spent some time in person and on the phone with them doing some coaching prior to the event. I had full confidence in these two young women to lead this event. While I desired to be at the event, my son's wedding took precedence.

Release

I've been praying for Susan to be able to minister alongside me, particularly with the young women on the team. With Maria, she had the opportunity, even though it was done on a phone call half a world apart.

Maria felt a strong calling to the Bible translation ministry, but she also had young daughters that were acting out over her absences from home due to the ministry. Yes, their grandmother was there, and a nanny was there; but Mom was not there, and the young daughters needed their mom. With the Gateway Language project complete and Maria transitioning to a new role, she was struggling with this tension. I spoke with her about it. Her male boss at BTS spoke with her, as well as a female colleague. Sierra was childless at the time, so none of us could relate to her as a mother and give her peace.

While Maria was struggling, Susan and I had a call with her. In the call Susan was able to validate her as a mother and give her the peace she needed, as well as the permission she needed. She resigned from the ministry shortly after that, and though I miss having her on the team, this season is for her to be with her children.

Maria was a person we didn't want to let go from the team, but there are some people that only participate for a season.

At the time she left, things were very strained in her marriage. In a few short months, after Maria placed the marriage at the foot of the cross and pleaded with God, significant healing has taken place. It is a blessing to hear what God is *doing* in growing Maria and restoring her marriage, and that the prayers that I and others made for her marriage to be healed have been answered.

Transitions can be challenging for both parties. I know we miss having Maria as a regular part of the team and she misses being a part of the team.

> *For everything there is a season, and a time for every matter under heaven.*[23]

Involuntary Transitions

As organizations change seasons, we sometimes find individuals in the incorrect roles. In some cases, particularly with smaller organizations, we may not have the correct new role for the person and then need to remove the individual from the organization. Over my lifetime, I've had to court martial soldiers under my command and terminate a handful of employees, many times having to fly to a remote office for the meeting. While this has been necessary, it has never been easy. The only easy transition was when I had an employee in the wrong role after a transition and we were able to find the right new role within the organization.

In this case, the individual was a person that I met in my first trip to Indonesia. At the time we met he was the outgoing leader of the commercial company we partnered with in Indonesia and was transitioning to a role as Indonesian Program Manager, responsible for

---

[23] Ecclesiastes 3:1

church networking. He also had been helping to build the dream team, a group of pastors working on the Bahasa Indonesian Gateway Language program. This individual was instrumental leading BTS in their formative years. He was also instrumental in introducing church leaders to MAST and supporting the language vetting as we started the first few hundred languages in Indonesia.

From a travel perspective, this transition was the most challenging I've faced. I believe people deserve the dignity of a face-to-face meeting. You would think starting a trip in the middle of the Pacific, it would be easy – I was already two thirds of the way there. Unfortunately, in the Pacific you regularly have situations where "You can't get there from here." On my flight back to Fiji, the Cathay Pacific flight attendant asked why I would fly through Hong Kong to get between Fiji and Indonesia. From Nadi, Fiji, to Manado, Indonesia, is a distance of 3800 miles, a 7-8 hour flight if such a flight existed. With available flights, the best I could do was Nadi to Hong Kong to Jakarta to Manado, a distance of about 8500 miles, and a good 35 hours of transit time – in each direction – quite similar to the transit time if I had started in America!

With the operations reorganization, we are moving to the next stage and giving further autonomy to Christov and the Bahasa Technology Solutions team. They have the formidable mission of equipping the churches of Indonesia to complete Bible translation for every language in Indonesia. To do this, the structure of the team changed dramatically, and unfortunately, there wasn't a role that was a fit for this person.

With the reconciliation a few months earlier, he was at peace with the transition, and the fact that we weren't renewing his contract. There was confirmation that the decision was the proper decision, so both parties were at peace.

I am the true vine, and my Father is the vinedresser. Every branch in me that does not bear fruit he takes away, and every branch that does bear fruit he prunes, that it may bear more fruit.[24]

In Scripture, we are taught that pruning must happen to produce the most fruit. We are entering a season in this ministry where we must maximize the fruit production. With the previous organization structure, we had two branches competing for the same nutrients. In both Indonesia and Papua New Guinea, I had to make a choice as to what branch to prune.

In the Indonesian case, it was an obvious choice. He was struggling on whether he was a senior pastor leading a church, a church leader pursuing a larger role with the denomination, and this role in Bible translation. With split allegiances in a season of needing full commitment, he wasn't the one to lead efforts for the nation. We needed a sold-out leader, fully committed to the mission – which we had in Christov – to lead us in this next season.

Sometimes we can do pruning by placing a person into a different role but being a small organization, it can be challenging to find or create that alternative role. In these cases, we have to just prune without regret.

For the team it was important to provide the vision moving forward – let the team know how the vine freshly pruned was prepared for this next season so the team didn't focus on the cuttings but on the fruit expected from the remaining vines.

---

[24] John 15:1-2

Chapter Six - Indonesian MAST

I've known of Sierra for several years, but only started working directly with her in April of 2018. She recently told me that when she first met me, I seemed very reserved and hard. Sierra was taught English and French by her grandmother at a young age and speaks impeccable English. She was a former cultural ambassador for Northern Sulawesi, the province she lives in, and traveled extensively internationally. She has a great love for Jesus and is called to the ministry.

Sierra shares she did not have a specific call from God or prophetic word that affirmed her calling. In the beginning there was anxiety and fear. Sierra read her Bible and kept finding verses of encouragement that helped her to press on. Over time she has found that God has molded her for this role. As she experiences spiritual attacks, she finds scripture that strengthens her.

I sometimes jokingly refer to Sierra as Mini-me, because as I would have coaching sessions with Sierra, we'd stumble upon a trait or situation that I struggled with myself, so after a while, we'd be talking about something, a challenge would come up, and then I'd say "Mini-me." We got a lot of laughs out of those similarities in personality and character. A lot of this similarity may come from each of us being the eldest child.

Commitment or Lack Thereof

One of the first working challenges with Sierra was her continual postponements of her wedding. Final count was five postponements, most because another translation training event was scheduled. There was a fair amount of teasing about this, but it shows the heart she has for the mission. To this day, I don't think Sierra and Edwin took their honeymoon; but with a baby on the way, I think they missed that opportunity.

Discouragement

In different locations, the enemy may choose different tactics for spiritual warfare. With Sierra and the Indonesian team, it is frequently the spirit of discouragement. We spent a fair amount of time working to develop systems for identifying the attack and responses to quench the attack. I eventually gave the team copies of the book *Spiritual Warfare for the End Times* by Derek Prince (Prince, 2017). The proclamation at the end of this book "My Testimony of the Blood of Jesus" was particularly useful in helping the team know their identity in Christ and that Satan has no power over them.

Throughout the region, the spirit of discouragement seems to be the first attack out of the spiritual warfare bag. We all feel unworthy to be doing the work that we are called to do – that is the exact reason that God has called us. We are the rejected cornerstones, we are the weak that God uses to make fools of the strong. Only through our weakness can His strength shine.

I was recently at an event in Fiji. We had some expat prayer intercessors at the event. One of the intercessors was gifted in prophecy and had gotten specific words for several of the attendees. Two young men helping facilitate the event matched the characteristics of the young leaders God provides for the ministry. The prophetic word for these men spoke directly to the discouragement that I've seen time and time again – that these are lies of Satan, and these men are perfectly equipped for what God called them to do. It was sweet to be able to relate the back story with the prayer intercessor, and then to help the young men see the significance of the message and pray over them. I saw Sierra a few days after these young men and was able to share with her how God encouraged these men in their new battle facing the spirit of discouragement, a discussion Sierra and I have had countless times.

Chapter Six

Discrimination

The staffing strategy in the region is to bring existing trained staff into a region and then raise up new disciples, new local leaders to replace them. As we started doing work in Papua, there was a lot of resistance to this, and we weren't moving fast enough for some of our Papuan staff. In my mind they were all Indonesians whether of Asian descent or Melanesian descent.

It seemed that the pushback on Indonesians was particularly harsh on the women of the team more so than the men. I had several coaching sessions with both Sierra and her Papuan counterpart.

As I've opened my eyes more, I am learning of the half century of human rights violations against the native Papuans. In the summer of 2019, there was a bad flare-up of violence between other Indonesians and Papuans, both in Java and Papua.

My lesson in this is that with deep rooted hurt it can be challenging to place Christian behavior ahead of tribal protection. It reinforces how desperate is the need for the Word of God in every language.

The Baby

Following her wedding, Sierra had a desire for a baby. This was one of the prayer points I had for her and her husband Edwin. Marrying later in life, there was concern it would be difficult, hence the call to prayer.

In August of 2019, I was in Indonesia for a staff retreat for the BTS team. Sierra wanted to talk to me and she told me she was with child. Then she asked me why I was crying. They were tears of joy for the answered prayer. I was very grateful Sierra waited to share the news with me until I was in in Indonesia with her.

I'm awaiting the next answered prayer for Sierra and her husband Edwin. Their desire is for Edwin's parents to become strong Christians and we have been praying for this. In Sierra's fifth month of pregnancy,

I had a short visit with Sierra, her sister Tessa, and brother Aim. Tessa and Aim have both been involved in MAST and both facilitated the Sawi event, though I had to intercede for Aim. Sierra was nervous about his participation, because a few months earlier he had contracted malaria at another MAST event in Papua. Aim loves Jesus and wants others to hear Jesus in their heart languages. Sierra was being the protective older sister to her baby brother.

During this visit with Sierra and her siblings, I was able to pray for the three of the siblings and Sierra's baby son as they dropped me off at the airport. I placed my hand on Sierra's hands as I was praying over her son, and she moved her hands so my hand was directly over the baby in her womb. As I'm praying, I started weeping in the Spirit as the Holy Spirit directed me to pray for Sierra's son to be the instrument to draw his grandparents, Edwin's parents, to Christ. It was a powerful, Spirit-directed prayer, and everyone in the car was weeping as I prayed. During the prayer, the baby started kicking up a storm, drumming on my hand. As I reflect on it, it's much like the reaction of John, leaping in the womb, as Mary arrived.[25]

As I reflect on working with Sierra, there are two primary lessons. First, as I look at Mini-me, where one of her character traits mirrors what I've experienced in the past, I find that much of personal transformation is from the fruit of the Spirit. It is only through the Holy Spirit that I've gotten the patience I've needed, the kindness and gentleness, the love. The second lesson is around dying to self and trusting in the Lord. Daniel 4:35 reminds us that God is in control of the heavens and the earth and what takes place in both realms. With our work in Bible translation, we see these two realms more clearly than most people. This ministry provides numerous opportunities for us to demonstrate our faith and trust. Sometimes we do well, sometimes we need more

---

[25] Luke 1:41

coaching. It's an honor to have the opportunity to disciple Sierra and to see myself in the mirror through her, and in that reflection the phenomenal transformation I've gone through with Christ Jesus.

Chapter Seven – The Papua Team
Yanti Monim

Yanti and I first met at the Papuan Malay New Testament event. We didn't communicate much because I spoke no Bahasa or Papuan Malay and she spoke very little English. My biggest impression was the joy she had.

To help Yanti with her English, we had her attend Orlando Exchange in 2018, a six-week English Language Learning course we host with our winter volunteer team. Susan was able to meet her during that trip while we were there for a Wycliffe Associates Board meeting, so Yanti is the one person on the Indonesian team that Susan has personally met.

We spoke recently about her calling. She told of a night that she had a prophetic dream. She was in a forest and there was a wolf pack with wolves from small to large. Yanti was fearful they would bite her arms and was quite afraid. God's voice told her "Do not be afraid. You will lead all the wolves from small to big out of the forest." When she awoke, she prayed and Psalm 23 came to her, and she sang it in Bahasa Indonesian.

> *The Lord is my shepherd; I shall not want.*
> *He makes me lie down in green pastures.*
> *He leads me beside still waters.*
> *He restores my soul.*
> *He leads me in paths of righteousness*
> *for his name's sake.*

Even though I walk through the valley of the shadow of death,
    I will fear no evil,
for you are with me;
    your rod and your staff,
    they comfort me.

You prepare a table before me
    in the presence of my enemies;
you anoint my head with oil;
    my cup overflows.
Surely goodness and mercy shall follow me
    all the days of my life,
and I shall dwell in the house of the Lord
    forever.[26]

After the dream, the Holy Spirit impressed on Yanti that her calling is not to comfort but to the areas of Papua with the greatest obstacles. She is to go into the danger zones.

This Psalm has repeatedly provided comfort to Yanti and the Papuan team. Last August the team made a 24-hour boat ride in an open boat from Timika to Asmat to facilitate an event with the Sawi people and two other tribes. There was five to six hours of heavy rain and rough water during the trip in the open boat. A few months later, at the Indonesian Prayer Summit, they sung the Psalm in the Papuan Malay language, in remembrance of how God had used it to comfort them during the storm on that boat.

Networking

For the past couple of years, Wycliffe Associates has been working to develop stronger partnerships with local church networks. Our desire

---

[26] Psalm 23

is to have partnerships that reach a wide swath of languages across a region, rather than building relationships language by language.

Yanti was a successful businesswoman in Papua, Indonesia. She ran a heavy construction company that built roads and bridges. I've had the privilege of traveling over some of these public works. This was part of the comfort Yanti had to give up – the income from running a successful construction company.

With her business background, Yanti is a strong networker and negotiator. In the summer and fall of 2018 I made three trips to Papua. While in Papua, Yanti, Christov, and I had a series of meetings with the major denominations. Yanti then started executing several partnership agreements with these denominations to work with Bahasa Technology Solutions and Wycliffe Associates. These agreements ensure every one of the hundreds of languages in Papua waiting for God's Word will have complete Bibles.

In addition to church meetings with Christov and me, Yanti had one stand-alone meeting in particular that stands out. She traveled on a flight with Associated Mission Aviation (AMA) to Bokondini in the highlands of Papua province. She was traveling with Pastor Dorman, the president of the Gereja Injili Di Indonesia (GIDI) (The Evangelical Church of Indonesia) denomination. When they arrived, fighting broke out in Bokondini, but Yanti and Pastor Dorman were able to diffuse the conflict and bring peace for the day. Later in the day, he had AMA fly Yanti back to Sentani. Despite Yanti not staying for the conference, Yanti and Wycliffe Associates were recognized as being the only Bible Translation organization willing to go despite the danger. Other invited organizations did not attend the event.

We're currently planting the fields with these partnerships and expect to see quite a harvest in the next two years. There has been tension in Papua for many decades since it was put under Indonesian rule, and

Indonesia continued a transmigration program[27] initiated by the Dutch. In recent months, this has led to protests and violence[28] in both Java and Papua. With the ongoing conflict in Papua, the harvest can't come soon enough.

Relief

In March of 2019, there was severe flooding and deadly mudslides in the cities of Sentani and Jayapura in Papua, Indonesia. A number of Wycliffe Associates leaders were just a few hundred miles across the border in Lae, Papua New Guinea, for a Great Commission Bible Translation Conference. As soon as we heard of the disaster, we were able to supply disaster relief funds to our local Papua team so they could help the translators that were impacted, as well as our partner church networks. Over a dozen active Bible translation projects were directly impacted by the flooding. A large number of families living around Sentani Lake had their homes flooded with up to 3 meters (10 feet) of water.

The local team in Jayapura started distributing the relief supplies; but through God's providence, we had a large contingent from the rest of the Indonesian team coming to Jayapura for team training, as well as a contingent from neighboring Papua New Guinea. By the weekend, the extended Pacific team was all pitching in to deliver these relief supplies.

Some would say this was simply a natural disaster, triggered by heavy rains and illegal logging in the surrounding mountains that contributed to mudslides. It is no coincidence that this also happened as we were working to equip a number of Papuan church networks with Train-the-Trainer training, along with about fifty other trainers from Indonesia and Papua New Guinea. We had a significant prayer

---

[27] https://en.wikipedia.org/wiki/Transmigration_program
[28] https://en.wikipedia.org/wiki/2019_Papua_protests

shield up ahead of the event, and the training event was able to be conducted without significant impact.

Pharisees

In the Gospels we see a number of occasions where Jesus is rejected or questioned because he is not doing things as the traditionalists expect. We also see Jesus getting angry, turning over tables of the money changers in the temple.

At one of our training events to equip national staff and church partners, there was an incident over views of appropriate dress. Just as a training session was starting, Yanti decided that Sierra's attire was unacceptable and publicly humiliated Sierra in front of the whole room. As I've worked with people from New Guinea, I find that some of them have anger that comes on in a flash. Sometimes it results in violence and killings, in this case it was "controlled" and merely resulted in Sierra being in tears for the rest of the morning.

With the battles we face with the enemy, I've developed a strong relationship with my staff, male and female. Sierra was hurting bad and needed to be consoled. She had the trust in me to help her through this. This is certainly the type of situation I would much rather have Susan handle, but it's kind of hard when her ministry is half a world away. Fortunately, one of our staff members and his wife was with us at this event. Cheryl was able to join me to pray with Sierra and help Sierra regain composure.

The situation was complex; and months later I would come to realize that there's 50 years of history feeding into the situation, a history that started before the birth of either Yanti or Sierra.

Later that day we had a session with Christov and his HR Manager, Pastor David, Sierra, Maria, Yanti, and me. We recognized a pattern of outbursts over various issues had affected Yanti's relationship with Maria and Sierra. Like many Papuans and Papua New Guineans, Yanti sometimes transitions quickly to anger, and you can read it in her eyes. This time, the excuse was attire, attire that I found no different than the attire of Papuan women attending the same session. I shared some scripture and shared my concern about discrimination from Yanti to her Indonesian sisters in Christ. I remember Yanti saying that if Maria and Sierra weren't suitably dressed, then the Papuan church would reject Bible translation.

Boom! The Holy Spirit burst out from me. I recalled images of Jesus turning over the moneychanger's tables in the temple, and I shouted loudly, "Pharisees, Pharisees," while pounding my fist on the table. I also spoke out "This is His land and He wants it clean." Yanti was shaken by this and left the meeting. On her drive home she shared that she was ready to quit, but God told her to go pray, so she went to her war room and prayed.

I was trying to get my arms around this as well. Outbursts like this aren't normal for me today; it was clearly the Holy Spirit. I joined the team for dinner but fasted and looked for the passage in the Gospels that was flashing through my head. John says:

> *That's when his disciples remembered the scripture, "I am consumed with a fiery passion to keep your house pure."*[29]

Things were becoming clearer. God was looking for a cleansing of the Papuan church. He wants the land cleaned and Satan evicted, but some of the powerful churches in Papua were like the Pharisees – all show without substance. Throughout the island, in both Papua, Indonesia, and Papua New Guinea, along with much of the rest of Melanesia, there is a long history of witchcraft, tribal fighting, cannibalism, and other evil. The nations claim to be Christian, but it is more a label than churches full of surrendered Christians. Where convenient,

---

[29] John 2:17 (TPT)

Christianity is practiced, where inconvenient, ancient practices surface. In some cases, prosperity gospel has also corrupted Christianity.

I have a mentor in Australia who is a long-time pastor – in his seventh decade of pastoring. John was introduced to us by a prominent Christian Indonesian business leader. The two men serve together in Indonesia, promoting David Pawson's book, *Unlocking the Bible* (Pawson, 2007). John's intro opened the doors to Vanuatu for Wycliffe Associates. I first met John and started to get to know him in Vanuatu a year ago. I called him shortly after this outburst and wanted to understand the outburst better. As I started talking, John explained his recent experience in Indonesia and how the Spirit has him "spewing." I didn't understand what spewing was, but as he explained, it seemed we were experiencing the same thing. The Holy Spirit was using this gentle man as a vessel for expressing righteous anger.

Reconciliation

I spoke of the reconciliation between my field operations peer and myself after our year-long conflict. We were in Indonesia with the entire BTS team in early August for a team-building session. I spoke with my peer and said, "I feel we should be transparent and talk about our conflict and reconciliation." The conflict was no secret to the staff – through numerous emails and other exchanges it was very public. We needed to make God's miraculous healing of the relationship equally as public, particularly with the strife between Sierra and Yanti.

We shared about what had happened and how God healed us. We then had a time of prayer. I found myself drawn to one of the Indonesian staff members, and he expressed that he felt I didn't like him. We prayed and as we were praying, I started weeping in the Spirit. We prayed until the Holy Spirit had healed things between us.

From there, my colleague felt called to start the process with Sierra and Yanti. The circle grew, and soon my prayer partner and I joined in praying and the five of us experienced the joy of reconciliation between Sierra and Yanti. A few days later we were at a retreat center; and as I was sitting on the bus to leave, I looked out and saw Sierra and Yanti having a conversation and embracing. We have a good, good Father, and His healing touch can mend any hurt.

During a recent trip to Manado, Indonesia, I spent a few hours with Sierra and her sister Tessa and brother Aim. It was a sweet time of fellowship. Later I received a hello text from Yanti and I mentioned I had lunch with her sister Sierra. She responded back that she also misses her sister in Christ Sierra. I shared that with Sierra and heard back "Praise the Lord. I miss her too and am so glad that all is well between us now."

Yanti is one on the team that I have a deep love for as my sister in Christ. She is also one that I have one of the most complex relationships with on the team. My desire to see all Papuans have scripture in their heart language can't possibly run as deep as Yanti's, given she is a Papuan, but the common calling has bonded us together. That bond has helped when things have been tough.

> *Pay attention to yourselves! If your brother sins, rebuke him, and if*
> *he repents, forgive him, and if he sins against you seven times in*
> *the day, and turns to you seven times, saying, 'I repent,' you must*
> *forgive him.*[30]

The Pharisees incident wasn't the only time God has called on me to guide Yanti through difficult challenges and to attempt to help her grow. That has caused periods where she loved me but I'm sure she didn't like me very much. I pray that my sincerity to serving Papua helps heal those wounds. I think God uses me because Yanti and I both still have a personality that can get in your face and not back down

---

[30] Luke 17:3-4

when it's hard. I would like to be operating with peace, patience, kindness, gentleness, and self-control all the time. As we saw when Jesus turned over the money-changer's tables,[31] His temple tantrum suggests there is a time for righteous anger.

Yanti has a deep conviction to get scripture into every heart language in Papua, an area with an estimated 500 languages. God called her to leave comfort and go to the areas with the greatest obstacles. She's been nearly lost at sea once and has taken rides in open boats where it stormed all night. She is not afraid of danger.

> *Now I want you to know, brothers and sisters, that what has happened to me has actually served to advance the gospel.*[32]

---

[31] John 2:13-16
[32] Philippians 1:12

Christov

Christov and Ferry were the first members of the Bahasa Technology Solutions (BTS) team I met in August of 2016. Christov was just coming into the role as Executive Director of Bahasa Technology Solutions, after a stint as a forensic accountant at the Jakarta offices of a big-four global accounting firm. Ferry was the outgoing director, transitioning to a program management role to develop relationships with churches for our MAST program.

Christov was young, joining the team at 25 years old, slightly younger than my younger son.

Christov was raised in the GKI Synod offices in Jayapura. His father and aunt were both very involved in the denomination and Christov spent many hours running the halls of the Synod offices. GKI is one of the largest two denominations in Papua, a mainline protestant denomination.

I asked Christov about his calling to the ministry. He shared how God had led him to this big-four accounting firm, where he was fast tracked, getting a double promotion in his last year at the firm. With his role, he was finding it increasingly difficult to maintain his integrity as a Christian while doing the work he was being asked to do. He prayed to God like Moses did in Exodus – saying he wouldn't move without God leading. If it were God's will, Christov would have stayed at the firm, but if not, God would have to open the door to his exit. In 2018 I met Jim Olsen, who was running a guest house in Sentani. Jim was a retired Bible translator and an accountant. Back in 2016, Jim answered Christov's prayer by reaching out to him after a three-year break in communications, to ask if he might be interested in helping with this business that supported Bible translation. Christov interviewed with the Global South Services Consultant and Pacific Regional Director at the time and was hired to lead Bahasa Technology Solutions. Christov shared how he uses interviews as a witnessing opportunity. In his exit interviews, he was speaking with one of the partners at the firm. The partner told Christov he can see how he was following God's lead and said, "I cannot counteroffer God." Interestingly, the partner was a non-believer.

Standards

The more I've experienced spiritual warfare in this work, the more convicted I am that we need a team of humble, obedient saints, who aren't perfect, but are quick to repent when they do fall. For all the leaders on the team, it is an ongoing coaching responsibility to raise the teams to the same level.

In spiritual warfare, sin creates opportunities or toeholds for the enemy to attack. I had an event in the Eastern Highlands of Papua New Guinea where I was unintentionally crushing the spirit of not one, but three other members of the team. I believe God provided that teachable moment for me to see how pervasive it was with me. I can tend to put mission above people and get so focused on results that I run over people in the process. Susan affectionately calls this my bulldozer mode. I repented to all three of the individuals. One of the individuals commented about my repentance being rare. He said that most people don't have the self-awareness and don't go to repentance so quickly. I told him that with spiritual warfare, if I see a sin, I have to repent quickly to close that toehold before the enemy can attack.

In Christov's case, he had hired an individual to help with information technology. In my getting to know the individual, the conversations suggested that this individual was not yet married but living with his fiancé. I passed that on to Christov, since it was his staff. He gave the person a pass, feeling the couple was almost married. A couple months later, there were multiple accusations of moral failure by this person involving several other individuals. From that lesson, Christov learned that a higher standard than society's was mandated and since has revised his policies.

There are two sides to this topic of sin. On the one side, the sin provides opportunities for the enemy to exploit. Pride is an easy one to exploit and is why God has assembled this team of broken, humble saints. We know the accomplishments we experience occur only through Him. Despite that, we sometimes forget and pride can appear. We must be vigilant to die to self daily. On the other side, avoiding sin opens the door to being Spirit filled and therefore, Spirit controlled. A. W. Tozer (Fant, 1964) warns:

> *Whoever would be indwelt with the Spirit must judge his life for any hidden iniquities. He must expel from his heart everything that is out of accord with the character of God as revealed by the Holy Scriptures.*

While this was a good teachable moment for Christov, as leaders, we must instill this in the entire flock to be properly equipped for these battles for eternity. The book *Spiritual Leadership* (Sanders, 2007) has great teaching on this topic, particularly the chapters "Essential Qualities of Leadership" and "Above All Else."

> *Pay careful attention to yourselves and to all the flock, in which the Holy Spirit has made you overseers, to care for the church of God, which he obtained with his own blood.*[33]

Tension and Agreeing to Disagree

In ministry, things aren't always clean. We don't always agree. Is it necessary for us to always agree? No, but we must have community. If

---

[33] Acts 20:28

we do not have full unity, we must be able to reason things out and at the end of the day have a common path forward.

Christov has been in a difficult position these past 3 ½ years. He clearly sees the vision of having a Bible in every language by 2025, but his role as director of BTS had been more administration for BTS than leading the efforts. Wycliffe Associates was leading the efforts and had three teams involved – the regional director responsible for church relations, the MAST director responsible for training churches and language groups in MAST, and the gateway language director responsible for running programs to translate scripture and helps into Bahasa Indonesian and Papuan Malay. Christov's team supplied contract workers to Wycliffe Associates for these three functions but the teams took operational direction from Wycliffe Associates. In some ways this model's flaws are obvious now, but at the time, it was how things had been set up with the best of intentions and goals.

Growth and Trust

I've had many interactions with Christov in these past 3 ½ years and have shed many tears with him and his family. Tears from misunderstandings and disagreements, tears from a deep-rooted compulsion on both our parts to see every language with scripture in the next five years. In this, we both have trust and respect for each other and know that we are both all in when it comes to the mission and vision.

Recently in my new role, I was able to release Christov and his team to be the primary entity supporting MAST in Indonesia. My management has said that this transition will require trust on my part, because I won't have direct authority, only influence. With the relationship, I'm not at all concerned. This is freeing up Christov and BTS to rise up to their full potential and no longer be constrained by inefficient structure and operating process imposed by Wycliffe Associates. We have our idea on how to do things; but ultimately, we don't have sufficient local context to do it properly by ourselves. It takes a partnership of strong local leaders and strong leaders from Wycliffe Associates with a common vision working as equals. We each have our strengths. We each have our weaknesses. But together we are the Body of Christ, and through Him all things are possible for this body to accomplish.

Immediately prior to the reorganization, I had asked Christov to outline how he thought BTS needed to be structured following the transition. I said dream big. Christov and others on the team had been praying in the weeks leading up to the transition. The answer to prayer was far better than they had been praying. So often as Christians we have specific requests to God, and what we ask for is so much less than He really wants to give us. God has entrusted over 700 known languages and, based on experience, probably well over 2100 total languages to Christov's team to equip and support for Bible translation in Indonesia. We believe He is calling us to finish the task in five years. Much like Jesus says in Matthew 18:3, we must be dependent like little children, have the faith of little children, and dream big.

Christov and I get to enjoy the same season of being entrusted with much.

> *His master said to him, 'Well done, good and faithful servant. You have been faithful over a little; I will set you over much. Enter into the joy of your master.'*[34]

While God is entrusting much to me, I know I can't do it alone. It's a pleasure having Christov in this key role beside me, leading the monumental efforts in Indonesia. It also comes at a good season where Christov has learned he can't do it himself. He has multiplied his team with solid leaders, including a number of pastors. These teams are each discipling and multiplying their respective teams.

---

[34] Matthew 25:23

Chapter Seven
Jhon Wesly (John Wesley)

Wesly is a Papuan who comes from a long line of strong Christians. His father is a pastor and was part of the team that translated the Papuan Malay New Testament in less than a week. His grandmother, who recently went home to the Lord, was a strong prayer warrior and prayed throughout Wesly's lifetime for him to serve the Lord as a missionary. I had the opportunity to meet his grandmother before she went home to the Lord, and I've preached in his father's church several times.

I asked Wesly about his calling, and this is what he said:

> When I grew up to be a teenager, I got it very clear deep in my heart that I will bring the mighty name of my Lord to my people of Papua. I will serve from one tribe to another tribe, bring the Good News of Salvation from my Lord, Jesus Christ, to my people of Papua.

> Now, when I am here with Wycliffe Associates and Bahasa Technology Solutions, I see what God had put in my heart since I was a teenager has been started to implement. This is my world. This is my real world. I am back to my real world after I did some other professional works.

> All glory only to my God, my Lord, and my King.

> I am His servant, I am only a dust and I am nothing before Him. But by His abundant grace, He gave me a big opportunity to serve Him. I am thanking God for that and will serve Him with all my heart and my strength and all my life.

Today Wesly is traveling to the far reaches of Papua, serving from tribe to tribe to bring the Good News from Jesus Christ to all the people of Papua.

Christov introduced Wesly to me in September of 2018 as a candidate for MAST coordinator for Papua and Gateway Language Coordinator for Papua. We wanted a MAST Team in Papua, but I wanted Wesly to focus on one job at a time. We needed the Gateway Language work completed in less than a year. This was an enormous task – equivalent to about 20 New Testament translations – with a goal of less than twelve months to complete the task. Also tasking Wesly with MAST coordination responsibilities could have been a mistake. Papua could have lost the opportunity to have these valuable resources to support every project across Papua. Wesly had a couple small distractions, but ultimately led the team to complete that monumental project two and a half months early.

To put this in context, there was an existing project for Papuan Malay being funded by another Bible translation organization. We had talked to the translation team for that alternate project about coming alongside them so that the effort could be accelerated to make it available as the source text for Papua. This opportunity to partner was declined. I recently came across a fundraising appeal on a website for this other Papuan Malay project. They were raising money for printing and digital programs in advance of completion of the Papuan Malay New Testament – which is targeted for 2028. This effort has been going on since at least 2012 – and it is still nearly a decade away. The NT is one quarter of the content of the Bible. Wesly's team translated the entire Bible from an open licensed Bahasa Indonesian version and went through three levels of affirmation. The first level of affirmation was by the translation team – typically four people translating and checking each verse; then affirmed by multiple church leaders and community members – and finally affirmed by leaders from many of the denominations across Papua. All of this was done in under a year, including translating a keyword dictionary, translation questions to help those doing heart-language translation, and translation notes. So what is taking the other Papuan Malay team perhaps 15 or more years to do, by empowering the local church, Wesly's team was able to produce twenty times the content in less than a tenth the time.

Joe Bruce

As a grandfather, I see God drawing me to children more and more. Wesly's second son was born earlier this year, and I had the blessing of preaching at Wesly's father's church the day Wesly's son was dedicated. We had part of the Papua New Guinea team, as well as part of the Indonesian team present for the dedication.

I didn't know about the dedication in advance, nor did I know the name his son was being given. He was dedicated Joe Bruce, after Bruce Smith and me. It is a great honor to be an eternal part of a brother in Christ, having his legacy named for you. I'd say it is a burden, also wanting that legacy to be a part of the Kingdom. That burden stands in the shadow of the far greater burden Bruce, Wesly, and I carry – to get God's Word to everyone called out in Revelation 7:9 – every tribe, every nation, every language, every people. I pray for Joe Bruce, but I also pray for every Melanesian and Pacific Islander that doesn't have God's Word.

At the recent Prayer Summit, I had a fair amount of time with Shema, Christov's one-year old daughter, including leading a presentation with her in my arms – maybe not the most professional, but as a Body of Christ, we are a family. There are many stories here on discipleship, but how young can we start? With Wesly away from home at the recent Prayer Summit, Joe Bruce was fussy one night. His older brother Mikhael, who is two, came over with his Bible and told his mom to please read so Joe Bruce can sleep. She did, and Joe settled down and went to sleep. After this, two-year-old Mikhael said, "Praise the Lord!"

*Train up a child in the way he should go;
even when he is old he will not depart from it.*[35]

Dry Bones

Following the overwhelming prophetic moment with Yanti, where I called out the Pharisaic behavior of the Papuan Church, Wesly invited me to provide the opening devotion for a gateway language event being held in Sentani the following week.

I am not a preacher, but when I let the Holy Spirit use me as his vessel, powerful messages can be delivered. In this case, God had me share about the dry bones in Papua, working through Ezekiel 31:1, 4 and 7-14, then talking about the early church in Acts 2:1-4, and the call for repentance in Acts 2:37-41. The message closed with Ezekiel 37:15-19 and Ephesians 2:15.

That weekend I had felt like Ezekiel because God was first using me to deliver hard messages and secondly using me as a vessel in bringing the Word of God to the barren land of Papua. Christianity existed, but it was hollow. Law and show had overtaken the message of salvation, of God's grace and mercy – primarily because they never had a chance to understand the message fully because the Word of God didn't exist in a language that spoke to their heart.

Wesly enabled this opportunity for God to use me in front of the church leaders that were doing the foundational work of the Papuan Malay translation. I had to decide if I would leave early or late that day for my evening flight out of Jakarta. Wesly convinced me to take the later flight and deliver the devotion as an encouragement to these Papuan leaders.

A few days later I was in Europe for the EurAsia Media and Distribution and Consultation Conference. I wasn't familiar with the Lauren Daigle song *First* (Mabury, Bentley, Fieldes, Ingram, & Daigle,

---

[35] Proverbs 22:6

2015), but that was a song the worship team led us in daily. That song crushed me, as I realized how little I really, truly put God first.

Before I bring my need
I will bring my heart
Before I lift my cares
I will lift my arms
I wanna know You
I wanna find You
In every season
In every moment
Before I bring my need
I will bring my heart
And seek You

[Chorus]
First
I wanna seek You
I wanna seek You
First
I wanna keep You
I wanna keep You
First
More than anything I want, I want You
First

Before I speak a word
Let me hear Your voice
And in the midst of pain
Let me feel Your joy
Ooh, I wanna know You
I wanna find You
In every season
In every moment

Pacific Saints

Before I speak a word
I will bring my heart
And seek You

God was preparing me for a new season. I was experiencing more visions and prophetic words, and more operating in the Spirit. With the increased gifting in prophecy, I began a quest this summer to deepen my knowledge of the Holy Spirit and deepen my intimacy with God. I had read *Forgotten God,* by Francis Chan, but really hadn't internalized it. It's interesting how God directs us – much like the story of Him directing those Muslims to Bibles in *Insanity of God* (Ripken & Lewis, 2012), God directed me to books on the Glory zone and on the Holy Spirit. In my case he appealed to my wallet – with free books showing up in the daily emails I received from Bookbubs and Page Chasers – two daily emails for discounted and free Christian books. This led to reading perhaps a dozen books on the two subjects, in addition to lots of related scripture.

In this ministry, I prefer to build the team with God's referrals rather than man's referrals. Due to this I started Wesly on the Papuan Malay project and had a lot of face time the first few events and had other trusted leaders alongside Wesly coaching him. Had I known the calling God placed on him, my fears would have been set aside; but I needed to discern this was God's choice and not Christov's choice. It was also a period of developing Christov. During that same time, Christov had hires that didn't work well.

Wesly is totally committed to the ministry. The coaching challenge now is to help him develop his team so he can go through the same process I did of equipping, empowering, and letting go. Wesly appears to be doing well in this transition, with the Papua team ready to break into three teams to serve Papua. This is just like Paul developing Timothy. It is called discipleship.

Chapter Seven

While he was still speaking to the people, behold, his mother and his brothers stood outside, asking to speak to him. But he replied to the man who told him, "Who is my mother, and who are my brothers?" And stretching out his hand toward his disciples, he said, "Here are my mother and my brothers! For whoever does the will of my Father in heaven is my brother and sister and mother."[36]

I'm proud to have Wesly as a brother.

---

[36] Matthew 12:46-50

Chapter Eight – The Papua New Guinea Team
Kenneth

K enneth and I first met at a Tok Pisin Gateway language event in late 2017, when he returned from the inaugural Great Commission Bible Translation Conference in Manila, Philippines. He is a well-respected pastor in the Evangelical Brotherhood Church of Papua New Guinea. He is also a Bible translator trained by the Summer Institute of Linguistics. He was the national leader of the Gadsup language project. There is another Pastor Kenneth on the team, but to keep things clear, I'll refer to the second Kenneth as Kautam.

Kenneth lives in a village outside of the Ukarumpa Station, a Summer Institute of Linguistics facility that hosts upwards of 500 missionary families. He had first engaged with MAST in some Open Bible Stories work for Gadsup and on the Tok Pisin project through the Bible Translation Association of Papua New Guinea (BTA).

Recently I learned of a prophetic word Kenneth received several years ago. There was a dedicated group of prayer intercessors from his wife's tribe, the Ontenu, who would pray regularly in the Ontenu village. I visited the village in June of 2018, before tribal fighting burned the last of the village to the ground. The women would pray in the Evangelical Brotherhood Church and sometimes God would give them a prophetic word. At this time, God gave them a word for Kenneth, it was from Isaiah 40:31 – having the wings of eagles. The essence Kenneth shared was "You will fly like a bird and travel widely." In 2018 Kenneth joined the Wycliffe Associates team and was quickly promoted to be the Assistant Regional Director, focusing on Melanesia. Since attending the 2017 Great Commission Bible Translation Conference in Manila,

Philippines, he has been in Fiji, the Philippines, Singapore, the Solomon Islands, and Vanuatu, as well as transiting Australia several times. Before this book is published, he will also make a trip to America. With all this flying, albeit on modern aircraft, he is certainly in the top three travelers in the region.

Goroka Tok Pisin - Martyrs

In November of 2017 we resumed the Tok Pisin project. This was the event where Kenneth and I met for the first time, but his reputation preceded him. In early 2016 we had started on the Tok Pisin gateway language project with the Bible Translation Association of Papua New Guinea (BTA), and Kenneth was a participant. In December of 2016, I met with BTA to discuss the continuation of the Tok Pisin gateway language project. Shortly after that meeting a letter was emailed to Wycliffe Associates, with copies emailed to essentially every Bible translation organization in the Pacific stating that BTA was rejecting MAST. BTA expressed still wanting to partner with Wycliffe Associates, but this November event they were given a specific opportunity that they rejected.

At this Gateway Language event we had a mix of Christian students that were part of the Tertiary Students Christian Fellowship (TSCF) and some pastors from across the highlands. The event started off well, but the second week the students did not return on Monday. I found out later that morning that they had been visited by their leaders from TSCF, dressed in suits, and were given a message.

The students were told by their peers that they were not qualified for the work. Several of the leaders shared they received images of the students being beheaded for mishandling God's Word. In God's providence I had been reading a David Jeremiah book on spiritual warfare (Jeremiah, 2016) and had been in Revelation 20 the previous night. Revelation 20:4 says that John saw the souls of those who had been beheaded because of the testimony of Jesus and for the Word of

God. Satan tries to be clever by speaking near truths. Here scripture talks of those beheaded from carrying the Word of God, Satan's associates tried discouraging by saying the beheading is due to mishandling the Word of God.

With help to see the truth of God's Word, these students were able to see this attack for what it was and regain confidence to begin translating again. There was lots of prayer with the students, Kenneth, and me in the process.

Two years later, one of those students is now a graduate and a key member of the BATTLE team in the Highlands.

Gadsup/Ontenu

In early 2018, Kenneth helped Wycliffe Associates pull together a MAST event for two of the Gadsup family of languages and the Ontenu language. In April we scheduled this event to take place in June. We had several of the Wycliffe Associates Banquet Directors attending as facilitators and Tabitha Price joining to co-facilitate and conduct MAST theory training following the event for our developing national staff, volunteers, and partners.

Two weeks before the event I received word there had been fighting in some of the tribes and there was risk for all the languages attending. I suspected it may be related to sorcery or *Sanguma*. I had learned about some of this when I attended a church conference in Papua New Guinea that April. When I shared about this with the American team and shared a recent National Public Radio (NPR) article[37] about it, I received feedback about not keeping the team up to date on the "News" in Papua New Guinea.

---

[37]   npr.org/sections/parallels/2018/05/24/612451247/in-papua-new-guineas-sorcery-wars-a-peacemaker-takes-on-her-toughest-case

Sanguma and witchcraft wasn't breaking news, this was common activity that had been occurring for decades, and the NPR article happened to be a current summary of the situation. Several of the expat participants questioned the wisdom of sticking with plans for the workshop. After review, it was determined that any potential threat was a tool for Satan and not a redirection from the Lord. The team boldly decided to forge ahead.

When we arrived in Papua New Guinea, we found that the pastor of the Ontenu Evangelical Brotherhood Church had died of cancer in April, about the time we booked the event. Unfortunately, superstition is common in Papua New Guinea and accusations that Pastor David had been poisoned or that a spell had been cast on him were made against two of the clans in the Ontenu tribe.

By that time there had been two major battles within the Ontenu tribe with several killings and about four dozen homes destroyed. Interestingly, at the MAST event, the Ontenu team was very committed to the process and translated more than the other two groups. Translators from both sides of the conflict were working side by side as teammates.

On the third day of the event, several translators received calls, asking them to return to the village for a battle scheduled for the next day. They all refused, saying this work was too important to interrupt.

The following day I received a vision in the morning of Susan and me standing at a celebration for the 100th completed MAST project in Papua New Guinea. It was a touching vision, given my desire to have Susan in the Pacific with me, and there was an immediacy with the vision, a sense that it would be in the next year or two.

That afternoon, we got word that the fighting had happened in the village and relatives of six of the translators were injured. Three of us – Kenneth, an American pastor, and I – joined the six translators and had a time of prayer to help them work through their grief and the spiritual attacks that might not have happened if they had gone to the village.

During the time of prayer, the American pastor prayed for the men to clearly see God's plans for Papua New Guinea. I had received that vision just hours earlier and started weeping hard – so hard my gut hurt.

Pastor Kenneth is the spiritual leader of the Ontenu (his wife's tribe), so he and several other pastors planned a visit to the tribe on Saturday. Tabitha, Tony, and the American pastor also wanted to go, so the Papua New Guinea pastors and the four of us made a visit to the Ontenu. We met with some additional pastors in the nearest town, Kainantu, and went in two groups to the Ontenu. Tony, Tabitha, and I went with one group to the main village while Kenneth, the American pastor, and Pastor Rodney went to the other village.

We were greeted by about five dozen armed men when we arrived. Things were clearly tense; yet, at the same time, life was continuing. That afternoon there was a Bride Price ceremony for an upcoming wedding, complete with two pigs. Women sat in the center of the village crocheting bilums while children played. It was amazing to me, how little fear they projected even in the middle of the threat.

Despite the tension in the two villages, the Holy Spirit preceded us and dictated the words out of our mouths. In both villages, He had us speaking words of God's love for the Ontenu and God's desire for peace. In addition, we had the first printed copy of the gospel of Mark in Ontenu to present to the tribe. After the presentation, Pastor Rodney invited us into his home for a traditional meal his wife had prepared.

Kassam #2 - Aiyugam Fighting

At the next event two months later, we had two new languages receiving training for the first time. Kenneth was back and we had Shilla facilitating her first event, after participating as a translator on the Ontenu project. As a young college graduate, Shilla is both humble and unassuming. At the June event she was the one person on the team who could type and had great planning and organization skills she used to serve the team.

This time Satan decided to strike at the Aiyugam tribe, Kenneth's own tribe. Some of his relatives were hurt in the fighting. I found Kenneth very upset as he was preparing to return to the village and remember praying for him. This was one of my turning points in accepting God's anointing as a pastor – when I need to provide comfort to other pastors.

I found later that Kenneth and others would only tell me the children's version of the events – I'd get that there was a killing or injuries in the fighting. They never shared the full graphic details of the brutality – the dismemberment of the bodies, the placing of body parts inside of other body parts. They didn't want to share with me the knowledge of those horrors.

Post Kassam #2 – Gateway Language Coordinator Hurt
In mid-2018, with the Tok Pisin Gateway Language project gearing up, I needed to transition to local leadership and take myself out of the day-to-day coordination of the project. I knew Kenneth had many irons in the fire; and though he was a Bible translator and a leader, I hadn't seen the hands-on management skills demonstrated that were required for coordinating the project. Because of this, Kenneth was not a serious candidate for this role.

I sent Kenneth an email after the event, informing him of the progress at the event and that I had selected Celsius as the Gateway Language Coordinator. I had talked with Kenneth and Misson (another member of his Gadsup team and a gateway language translator) about their desire to form a team to take MAST throughout the Highlands. In the email I also encouraged Kenneth that I would support Misson and him if they wanted to move forward with taking MAST to the villages of the Highlands.

Shortly after I sent that email, I received a short note back from Kenneth that he was very upset, that he felt the job should have been his. I also got pushback from our Papua New Guinea Program Manager that I hadn't consulted the national team. This letter was deeply upsetting to me. I felt Kenneth was a brother, and over a series of spiritual warfare battles we had spent much time in prayer as these spiritual attacks persisted.

Ephesians tells us:

> *For we do not wrestle against flesh and blood, but against the rulers, against the authorities, against the cosmic powers over this present darkness, against the spiritual forces of evil in the heavenly places.*[38]

These weren't just emotional attacks – people were dying. The spirit of death is something that we see consistently at most of our Papua New Guinea MAST events, particularly if there's been a long legacy of tribal fighting in the language communities involved.

In making my selection for gateway language coordinator, I had a long conversation with another national leader about what I was looking for, why I felt Celsius was the right person, and why Kenneth was not. Sometimes we are so busy with good, the great evades us, and that was Kenneth – he was spiritual leader of the Aiyugam and Often tribes, his and his wife's people. He was also a pastor and a key leader of the Evangelical Brotherhood Church denomination in Kainantu. He was still involved with the Gadsup project with the Summer Institute of Linguistics. He was also the father of five, with the youngest still a

---

[38] Ephesians 6:12

toddler. The combination of these responsibilities left no room for the Tok Pisin role.

The field operations team looked at alternatives that might be better suited to Kenneth, and he was brought on the team in a different role.

Recently I had Kenneth tell me that he now sees that he was not the right person for the job and is very happy that Celsius took on the role.

Release and Repentance

I talked about Kenneth's responsibilities with the Aiyugam and Gadsup tribes, two tribes that have been in conflict for well over a year. When the two of us were together in Fiji in October of 2019, a prayer intercessor at the event got a word for Kenneth. The word said, "God is raising up young leaders in your village in your absence even now. He is moving in their hearts, multiplying your influence on them so that they are a greater force than one man. They are like a quiver of arrows to fight this spiritual battle; you do not fight only with flesh and blood, but the spiritual forces of wickedness in the heavenly places. The quiver of young leaders will lead the reconciliation you have prayed for. God will bring peace to your people as they repent and turn to Him. He will use the next generation of leaders to bring it to pass."

The prayer intercessor, Celsius, and I shared this word with Kenneth, and he shed tears of joy, knowing that God was preparing others to lift this burden from him. We embraced and prayed for Kenneth.

Over the next couple days, an amazing transformation took place in Kenneth. He shared about how during a celebration of remembrance at his church less than a month prior, he was preaching and his son saw a tree rise up behind him with lots of leaves and light flickering in the tree. While this was happening, a bolt of light like a comet flew out from the tree and struck Kenneth's son. He was knocked out and had to be taken back to the house.

As I reflected on this, I was wondering if this was an anointing by the Spirit of Kenneth's son. I've asked Kenneth to test for new gifts of the Spirit in his son. This may be one of the young men the word was talking about. Kenneth shared with me when I saw him a few weeks later that his son's behavior is greatly improved. Nothing like a bolt of white light from the Holy Spirit to correct a 14-year-old and bring him in line.

Kenneth is not welcome in his village. As an ambassador of God's peace, he is working to resolve an ongoing conflict that others don't want to end. Frequently these conflicts continue until everything is destroyed and no one has anything left. A bridge to the village washed out recently and was repaired, but Kenneth was told he cannot use the bridge. While we were in Fiji, another young man in the village reached out to Kenneth and said that when Kenneth returned, this young man would broker a meeting to get Kenneth permission to use the bridge.

The story doesn't end with the relief over the word given to Kenneth. As Kenneth talked with Celsius and me about the Holy Spirit and this experience, Celsius and I were asking him about his relationship with the Spirit, had he been baptized in the Holy Spirit. As he shared, he talked of his bitterness over what he has faced. I have heard parts of the story about how he has had to go into the villages after a killing and gather up body parts so a proper burial can be done, stories of negotiating so the villagers can be laid to rest in the village. Kenneth carries a big burden and because of it, he has accumulated a lot of bitterness.

This had me weeping in the Spirit and I spoke out that he needed to repent for grieving the Holy Spirit. We prayed with Kenneth and he repented for the bitterness. It was interesting to watch the transformation of Kenneth. I look forward to seeing how much more effective Kenneth becomes as he grows in the Spirit.

Father, I acknowledge the reality of who I am. I acknowledge the weakness, the sin, the mess in my life and I ask you to come and have mercy on me, just as I am, because of who Jesus is.

So with your help I take my sin, my weakness, my pain, my grief and place it all on the cross where Jesus died, so that he can carry it away and then forget it forever. I let go of these things now.

With your help I choose to let go of grudges and bitterness and forgive all who have wounded me.

Father, would you please put the Spirit of Jesus deeply within me and begin to shape me and refine me? Will you begin to do what I cannot do? Will you begin to produce within me the person you've always wanted me to be? Will you please begin to lead me in the paths you've always planned for me? I ask this in Jesus' name. Amen. (Godwin & Roberts, 2012)

As I reflect on my relationship with Kenneth, it leaves me speechless. Kenneth is a very respected pastor, yet God has allowed me the privilege on multiple occasions of praying for him as a man, helping lift his human hurts. God has also allowed Celsius and me to mentor Kenneth as he works to strengthen his relationship with the Holy Spirit. Kenneth subsequently told me that nobody had ever asked him if he had been baptized in the Spirit.

And he said to them, "Did you receive the Holy Spirit when you believed?" And they said, "No, we have not even heard that there is a Holy Spirit."[39]

---

[39] Acts 19:2

Chapter Eight

Kenneth and I get to work as brothers fulfilling the Great Commission. We get to travel to the ends of the earth together. We get to lean on Celsius in learning how to better operate in the Spirit.

Shilla – Warrior and Saint

S hilla and I first met at the Kassam MAST event, where she was a translator for her Ontenu language. A petite young woman, we were impressed with her organizational skills and leadership, even at a young age. From that event we asked her to join the MAST Theory Training the following week. As I have gotten to know her across nearly a dozen events in three countries in the last 18 months, her inner strength continues to amaze me.

Shilla's grandfather was a big influence on her life, and he sent her to college with the expectation that she could help with the administration of his coffee factory. After college Shilla was looking for work. She attended one of the Ontenu prayer meetings. She asked for prayer as she was preparing to put out some job applications. One of the vessels (a Papua New Guinea mama or woman with a gift of prophecy) prophesied that Shilla would not work inside the office but would work outside and in the field. With her work bringing Bible translation to remote villages, this prophecy certainly has been fulfilled.

Not Good Enough

Some time after Shilla started volunteering with Wycliffe Associates, I found that she had applied for a position with a national Bible translation organization in Papua New Guinea. She had been turned down for the position because she wasn't qualified. I am so grateful she was rejected, because she is having enormous impact on Bible translation in the Pacific, teaching and equipping dozens of language communities so far in Papua New Guinea and elsewhere – far more impact than she would have ever had on Bible translation elsewhere.

Chapter Eight

Madang #1 - The Battles

I remember talking with Shilla at the second Kassam event about her tribe and the ongoing conflict. Immediately before this event, she had been going to the village to deliver food to the men living in the bush. Shortly after our June workshop the remainder of the village was destroyed and the men were staying to protect her grandfather's coffee factory and the plantations that hadn't yet been destroyed. Practically every event saw more violence erupt within her tribe.

I didn't attend the Madang event because my son Jonathan was getting married. He saved me having to make a tough choice between the Sawi event in Papua and the Madang event in Papua New Guinea. Even though the Sawi event was an unprecedented event, if I knew then what I know now, I would have gone to the Madang event if not for the wedding.

During the Madang event Shilla received a phone call from her grandfather that his coffee factory and coffee plantations had been destroyed, and the remaining houses had been burned down. It was heartbreaking to her, and she desperately wanted to be home with her family. Depending on road conditions, it can be a 5- to 12-hour drive between Madang and Kainantu. Her uncle sent her an encouraging text message from the capital city of Port Moresby with a quote from Hebrews 12:2:

> *We look away from the natural realm and we fasten our gaze onto Jesus who birthed faith within us and who leads us forward into faith's perfection. His example is this: Because his heart was focused on the joy of knowing that you would be his, he endured the agony of the cross and conquered its humiliation, and now sits exalted at the right hand of the throne of God!*[40]

---

[40] Hebrews 12:2 (TPT)

Shilla is a fighter and with a broken heart she prayed to God. *"God you bring me here to help your people in Madang to translate your word into their own tongue and this is the first week of this workshop. I don't wanna quit this workshop and go help me and give me strength and courage to continue on with the workshop, Make me forget about all the terrible things that happen in my village and to my grandfather's property, help me to focus on your work. I also pray to God to help my grandfather forgive those who destroy his property."*

The next day her grandfather called her and said *"I forgive those who done this terrible thing to my factory."* This was an answered prayer for Shilla, and she had peace the remainder of the workshop. She told Tabitha, *"I put my hope in Hm. I know Satan will not dictate my destiny for I believe in God - He is the living reality."*

The Firsts

Shilla is a young lady, still in her early 20s. While she did go to college in Goroka, prior to her involvement, she hadn't traveled much beyond Eastern Highlands province. It's been a joy to share some of her firsts – the first airplane flight, the first time on a motor boat, the first time crossing an international border, the first time flying to a foreign country. While there's a certain fear in her as she faces some of these novel situations, she has inner strength and commitment that most will never understand or personally experience. God is using her mightily, both within Papua New Guinea and across Melanesia.

Madang #3 – Steamrolled & Dejected

At the third Madang event, we had a prophetic moment where one of the mamas was used as a vessel to deliver a message. This translator had fallen during the worship to a fetal position. A short time later she started crying out for repentance. Shilla was next to me during this and there was one point that the Holy Spirit had me on my knees, weeping in the Spirit for repentance. This weeping wasn't pretty but didn't faze Shilla in the least.

Following this, I asked Shilla for further clarification of all that had happened. This took place in the Tok Pisin and other languages, and though I have been picking up some Tok Pisin and could get the general sense of what was happening, a lot of details were missing.

As we talked further, I asked Shilla if this was the first time she had seen a prophetic word delivered like this. She shared about the Ontenu prayer meetings her mom attended, like the one where Kenneth got the word on God's calling for him. She begged her mom to be able to attend these prayer meetings. At one of them, some time before Pastor David had died, one of the vessels spoke out about the Ontenu village being steamrolled. At the time she shared this with me, her village had been flattened and burned to the ground for almost nine months. I asked her what it was to fear God when you hear a prophecy like this and then live through it. It really was like some of the Old Testament prophecies we read about God's wrath for wayward people. The prophecy did have a redemptive phase to it, and we are still waiting to see that part of the prophecy fulfilled. Kenneth's brother-in-law Bayaka is the Ontenu elder who is the key holder – he determines if the tribe is in peace or conflict. Both Kenneth and I have reached out to him and pleaded for peace and pleaded for him and his warriors to put their energy into forging new weapons – the sword of the Spirit in Ontenu, by participating in the Ontenu Bible translation project.

Shilla and her cousin Bradley were doing some of their own weeping at this event, feeling dejected. We had recently conducted a TENT training event to train trainers that would lead MAST workshops in villages across Madang province. With these 25 trained leaders, Shilla and Bradley, a frequent volunteer facilitator, found they had been replaced as facilitators. This is the position we all must get to. I've done it multiple times across the Pacific, starting in a country, building up a team, and then as an expat, turning the responsibility over to nationals. Here was one of the first times within Papua New Guinea this was happening, where the nationals in one region had trained up nationals in another region, and it was time to let go. This was the first time Shilla and Bradley were experiencing the letting go. This letting go is a natural part of discipleship, when our disciples are ready to move out on their own.

With hundreds, if not thousands, of languages in Papua New Guinea, Shilla wasn't out of a job, she just had to accept that she could no longer be a part of every MAST event in Papua New Guinea. In the first half of 2018, westerners were still leading MAST in Papua New Guinea and a MAST event would happen every couple of months. As of the second half of 2019 – a mere 18 months later – Papua New Guinean teams were running in all four regions of Papua New Guinea: Momase, the Highlands, Southern, and New Guinea Islands. These teams are quickly progressing to multiple events in each region every month. There's no way anyone other than God could be omnipresent. Only God can be at all of the events at once.

Shilla has many fans among the Wycliffe Associates staff and volunteers that have worked with her in Papua New Guinea. Though she desperately wants me to be able to converse with her in Tok Pisin, she communicates well in English. It has been a joy watching her world expand as she had bucket list experiences such as leading MAST in a foreign country.

I think what most intrigues me about Shilla is the contrast between her rapidly expanding world and her conviction for the ministry and steadfastness in battle. She demonstrates such inner strength in the spiritual battles. While she may exhibit some fear and anxiety in turbulence on an airplane or on rough seas on a small boat, she doesn't show fear under fire in spiritual battles.

Chapter Eight

Therefore take up the whole armor of God, that you may be able to withstand in the evil day, and having done all, to stand firm.[41]

---

[41] Ephesians 6:13

Misson

Misson is part of Kenneth's Gadsup team that I first met in late 2017 at the Tok Pisin MAST event in Goroka. Misson has a big infectious smile behind his beard. Misson was working with the Bible Translation Association of Papua New Guinea as a volunteer literacy trainer.

I asked Misson about how he got here – the back story behind my bringing him on the team. Prior to 2012, Misson served with his Seventh Day Adventist church as a choir leader. In 2012 he started serving with the Summer Institute of Linguistics, teaching at literacy workshops. By 2014 he was dissatisfied that he was inadequately serving the Lord and frustrated with the infrequent literacy training events. He cried out to the Lord, "God, place me where I can serve you." At the same time, his wife was asking him to just stay home and help with the garden. Like many living in the Highlands of Papua New Guinea, Misson and his family were living in a traditional village home and the family raised crops to feed the family.

Following this initial prayer to more fully serve the Lord, Misson started working with the Gadsup translation team, helping on the New Testament translation project with BTA.

In 2016, Misson's wife attended a woman's conference in the community. At this event, each woman pulled a promise card from a basket. Misson's wife couldn't read, so she brought the verse home and asked Misson to read it to her.

Chapter Eight

Hope deferred makes the heart sick, but a desire fulfilled is a tree of life.[42]

This verse resonated deeply with Misson – he was in the season of deferred hope – crying out to the Lord.

Misson was a steady participant in the Tok Pisin Gateway Language project, and in February of 2019, I asked him to lead the project. This was the answer to his prayer—he felt convicted and immediately accepted.

Following this, as he studied the full extent of the job description, he felt overwhelmed and questioned that God would pick him up from nothing to lead this big program. He doesn't have a degree, he hasn't run a business, he is a simple man, but he has a heart to serve the Lord; and as Matthew 22:37 commands, he loves the Lord with all his heart, soul, and mind. He sees how God developed him as a teacher during his time as a literacy worker to give him the teaching skills necessary to lead MAST.

Misson experiences great joy in serving instead of resting. He sees that we are fulfilling Revelation 14:6

Then I saw another angel flying directly overhead, with an eternal gospel to proclaim to those who dwell on earth, to every nation and tribe and language and people.

To him, MAST represents the swiftness of flight – MAST is allowing the Gospel to be swiftly translated into all the languages of his nation.

---

[42] Proverbs 4:12

Kassam #2 – Bible Translation Club

At the second Kassam event, we spent one week at the Yonki Evangelical Brotherhood Church training center and the second week back at the Kassam Evangelical Brotherhood Church training center. I remember sitting in the dinner tent and listening to Misson share of the talks he and Kenneth had about forming a translation club and working to get Bible translation done across the Highlands. A little background will create context for understanding the significance of this conversation. A couple months earlier, I was talking with Bayaka in the Ontenu village, he shared about how his ancestors in 1954 sold their bush (forest land) to foreigners so they could log and use the lumber for the construction of the Ukarumpa Station. There was an expectation that Ontenu would soon get their Bible. When I visited in 2018, 64 years had passed and not a word of scripture was ever translated into the Ontenu language. The younger generation was questioning why their ancestors had made such a bad deal with the white skins.

Misson had a passion for reaching all the languages in the Highlands, and the Bible translation club was how God was giving him that vision. I asked him why he held back when I told him Wycliffe Associates could help him fulfill that vision. He said after that conversation, he spent a couple weeks drafting that plan in black and white on paper and shared the plan with Kenneth. Kenneth was his mentor as leader of the Gadsup project. Kenneth didn't feel it was time and discouraged moving forward.

Really, it was only a short six months between that conversation and Misson joining the team, when he had been crying out to the Lord for an opportunity to serve him for about five years – sixty months—so he was nearly at the finish line. The situation with Kenneth feeling passed over for the GL role when Misson presented the plan may have complicated things, but this is human analysis. Truthfully, it was in God's perfect time.

Chapter Eight

Yes

I had several conversations with both Kenneth and Misson about this Bible translation club. It was clear he was committed to continuing his work with the Summer Institute of Linguistics to help advance the literacy of the Gadsup people. In February of 2019 I found myself in need of a MAST coordinator for Papua New Guinea, after having to remove the previous coordinator in December. Celsius was an ideal candidate, but I would then need to backfill Celsius's role as gateway language coordinator. This time Kenneth endorsed my selection for gateway language coordinator, as Misson moved into the gateway language role and Celsius moved into the national MAST coordinator role.

Boldness

One of the things I appreciate about Misson is his boldness in speaking out. It is funny, because overall, he is quiet like most Papua New Guineans; but when he sees something that can be improved, he speaks out. We had done some training in Sentani in March and following the training, Misson explained to me how Papua New Guineans like to have handouts right in front of them during lectures. It shouldn't have surprised me, I'm more of a visual than oral learner myself.

The feedback on the training was just one of several things that Misson has brought to my attention. He is thorough; he creates solid end-of-event reports and financial reconciliations; he's a good manager, in addition to his God-given gifting as a teacher.

What I've discovered in Papua New Guinea is people like Misson are rare. Celsius will be the first to tell you that his pastoring skills don't extend to administration. With the education system, skills of graduates tend to be narrower than we see with graduates in America, Europe, or even Indonesia. It's not a reflection of the intelligence of the people, it's a reflection of the type of education.

To each is given the manifestation of the Spirit for the common good. For to one is given through the Spirit the utterance of wisdom, and to another the utterance of knowledge according to the same Spirit, to another faith by the same Spirit, to another gifts of healing by the one Spirit, to another the working of miracles, to another prophecy, to another the ability to distinguish between spirits, to another various kinds of tongues, to another the interpretation of tongues. All these are empowered by one and the same Spirit, who apportions to each one individually as he wills. [43]

I get to see the Body of Christ in action in this team. Misson has a gift as a teacher, but also has a strong calling to speak the truth in love. He is a quiet, gentle man, but a piece of bedrock on the team. He also gets to see God use him beyond his dreams. He had a dream of a club to lead Bible translation in the Highlands. He is seeing God use him not just in the Highlands but also across Papua New Guinea and other Melanesian nations.

---

[43] 1 Corinthians 12:7-11

Chapter Eight
Celsius

Celsius met me at a June 2018 event; however, I met so many people, I didn't really remember him. I remembered so little that at the August event I called him Cornelius. I'm not great with names, and many months I am meeting hundreds of new people. It can be overwhelming. I eventually got it right with Celsius when I realized he was one of the better dressers and frequently wore a light-colored shirt with flames up the sides. Hot dresser -> heat -> Fahrenheit -> Celsius – Got it. At the August event it was clear he was a leader. I was needing someone to take over coordination of the Tok Pisin gateway language project and asked him to consider the role.

In talking with Celsius recently, we discussed some of the early prophetic words he received that were answered with his call to this ministry. In 2007 he received a word that he would rise up as a leader in the land but would face many challenges much like Daniel in the book of Daniel. Later he received a word: *Do not be fixed but be open, God will take you beyond the local church.* Celsius was pastoring a small church in a small community with many other churches when he connected with Wycliffe Associates in 2018, more than a decade after that first prophetic word. In this past year, he has risen up to be the national leader of church-based Bible translation in Papua New Guinea, a land of many nations, many languages, where the most conservative estimates are 870 languages, but the reality could very easily be 2000-3000 distinct languages needing unique Bibles in the next five years.

Frequently we get asked about the difference between languages and dialects. When I have asked a speaker, they never refer to what they are speaking as a dialect. They always refer to it as their language. I was recently a guest speaker on a local Christian radio show that broadcasts in the southern Vermont and Capital Region of New York. Dan, one of the regular personalities on that show was sharing about how God talked to him in slang when he first came to Christ. That was Dan's language, and that was the language God used to speak to him. God cares about each of our individual languages and wants to speak to us in that specific language.

Alone

As Celsius and I got to know each other, it was pretty clear he felt he was the only person operating in the Spirit on the team. The rest of the team, myself included, were more mainline evangelical Christians, and many of us either resisted the Holy Spirit, as Kenneth had, or had not regularly sought the filling of the Holy Spirit. Many denominations don't embrace or teach Baptism in the Holy Spirit. It was easy to have conversation with Celsius about the spiritual warfare the team was facing. He shared that he felt alone in the beginning, being the only one operating more fully in the Spirit. It's been a joy to him as I have grown in the Spirit this past year and a half. The unity of the team has strengthened as we all continue to grow in the Spirit.

In the time since Celsius has come on the team we have had a lot of time for fellowship and prayer. I've made at least ten trips to Papua New Guinea and been with Celsius. Kenneth, Celsius and I traveled together to Vanuatu in December of 2018. We traveled together to Indonesia in March of 2019. We served together in Fiji in October of 2019. Some months I spent more time with Celsius and the team than I did with my wife. I've met his wife Joyce several times; she prepared a nice mu-mu (dinner cooked in the ground by heated stones) for us in Madang, and a wonderful lunch on a stopover at their home in Yonki traveling from Goroka back to Madang, and on a separate trip to Goroka. She's never met Susan but loves on her just the same and has sent her several beautiful bilums. We pray for Joyce's health issues to be resolved so she and Celsius can have children.

Chapter Eight

Kassam #2 - Flames on Pages

At the Kassam event that Celsius rose up to be identified as my Tok Pisin Gateway Language Coordinator, we had one pastor, Pastor Alkin, that got sick during the event and was diagnosed and treated for tuberculosis. I was surprised to see Pastor Alkin right back at the work, but he told me the work was too important to miss, and he had the medication he needed to get well.

On the last day of the event Pastor Alkin told me he had a dream, and he never has dreams that he can recall. In this dream, the Tok Pisin work was complete and all the pastors had open copies of the Bible in their hands. Dancing off the pages were flames, but the paper was not consumed.

I saw this dream as God telling us that these words would go out to all the lands so people could hear God in their heart language. That Tok Pisin Bible is the key to unlocking heart language translations into hundreds of languages across Papua New Guinea. Just like in Acts chapter 2, where the Holy Spirit descended upon the disciples and then thousands came to know the Lord after hearing the disciples speak in tongues, the Tok Pisin Bible was to be how the Holy Spirit talks to hundreds of languages, helping unlock God's Word into these languages.

Wycliffe Associates puts out a monthly glossy newsletter "eInvolved" and is seeking stories from the field to encourage our prayer partners and donors. In April of 2019, the marketing team was finishing an article about this incident of the burning Bibles vision and was looking for pictures of Pastor Alkin. I happened to be in Papua New Guinea, so Celsius and I took an overnight trip from Madang to Goroka. At 180 miles, you'd expect it to be a 3-hour drive or so, but with the conditions of the highways in Papua New Guinea, this was a 10-hour trip each way. Pastor Alkin is based in Goroka, so we were able to meet him at his church and take some pictures for the newsletter. It was encouraging to the three of us to recall that story and have a short time of fellowship and prayer. I later brought several dozen copies of that newsletter to Vanuatu and handed it off to Shilla to take back to Misson and the Tok Pisin Gateway Language team. I received feedback on how encouraging it was to the Tok Pisin team to see the article and corresponding weekly prayer points for Papua New Guinea that go out to the WA donors and prayer partners.

Must Pray – Prayer Warriors

It is always interesting watching God's plan unfold. Celsius and I had several conversations about the centrality of prayer to all we do. As we faced spiritual battle after spiritual battle, it all circled back to how well we were preparing through prayer and praying continually throughout the event.

At one point I was back home and called Celsius in Papua New Guinea to ask him what he thought of us scheduling Americans to come to Papua New Guinea as prayer intercessors. He said he had been thinking the same thing. I then started engaging our recruiting department, and they had been having the same conversation. They also referred me to Mickey White, who shepherded our Spiritual Disciplines work within the Education Services department. God had placed on four different groups of people in Papua New Guinea, Vermont, and Florida the same desire to start a field prayer intercession ministry in conjunction with the MAST events.

Sorry. Sorry, Sorry.

One of the barriers I have to deal with as an American, is I am white. My brothers in Christ in Melanesia have a long history of being under white rule. Frequently Celsius and I will be interacting and he will start saying sorry to me. These apologies are typically over trivial things like having a question for me. I have been trying to say we are equals, he does not have to apologize for interrupting. After the reminders, we get into sorry, sorry mode – apologizing for saying sorry. Even though I am the leader, when I'm with Celsius, I am there to serve him.

When are the experts arriving?

In late September of 2019, the first MAST on New Britain Island took place. Misson and the team went out early to prepare for the event and Celsius was arriving later in the weekend. As Misson and the team prepared for the event, the question was asked, "When will the experts arrive?" Misson responded that Celsius will arrive tomorrow. When Celsius arrived, there was great disappointment. The expectation was that white missionaries were coming to teach MAST, not Papua New Guineans. Celsius reassured them by telling them no experts were coming, the experts were not needed.

Celsius is a very generous man, and Susan and I have been the recipients of that generosity far too often. I've had to accept that tempering his generosity takes away some of his pleasure.

I think one of the giftings of Celsius is apostleship. He gets the mission and is carrying the mission across Papua New Guinea and out to Melanesia alongside Kenneth. The two complement each other. It is a blessing to have Celsius focused in Papua New Guinea and Kenneth focused on the rest of Melanesia, but at the same time having the two of them alongside each other, particularly when I can't be there. Kenneth is more the shepherd, Celsius more the apostle.

> *And God has appointed in the church first apostles, second prophets, third teachers, then miracles, then gifts of healing, helping, administrating, and various kinds of tongues.*[44]

---

[44] 1 Corinthians 12:28

Patrick

Patrick was introduced to me in December of 2018 by some leaders who were recommending him as a Papua New Guinea MAST coordinator. This was not a position I was going to interview for and fill. I had to see that this was a God-anointed position.

I asked Patrick how he got called. His wife Regina is a pastor's kid, and Patrick drove and served as Reverend Maka's assistant for ten years before Rev. Maka was called home to the Lord.

In 2015 a delegation from Papua New Guinea travelled to America to receive a first edition printing of the 1611 King James Bible that now resides in the House of Parliament in Port Moresby and was visited by Vice President Mike Pence last year. Rev. Maka was part of the delegation to the United States, and when he was there, he received a smaller Bible. Upon his return he gave that other Bible to Patrick.

In 2016 Reverend Maka went home to the Lord. Patrick then found himself looking for where the Lord was leading him next. He stayed involved in ministry and organized a youth camp in Port Moresby that was the largest ever in the country. In 2018 Patrick received an email from his secular boss telling him he was fired. This was the day before his birthday and was quite unexpected. He and his wife Regina went to Vision City, a large mall in Port Moresby to have dinner, pray, and process what had happened. While he was there, Regina's cousin passed my business card to Patrick, saying there was an opportunity with Wycliffe Associates.

Given the unexpected nature of the termination, it took some time for Patrick to process and come to peace with the termination. Patrick and Regina prayed for a couple of months and Patrick finally surrendered and forgave his former boss. He followed up at a time when I was in town for a Prayer Summit with the Papua New Guinea team, so I was able to meet with Patrick and have the first discussion about joining the team.

Wait for the Lord;
be strong, and let your heart take courage;
wait for the Lord![45]

Madang #2 - One Tok

One of the questions in Papua New Guinea always is why is this person recommended? We certainly want the best person possible in each critical role and want people that God is calling.

I had Patrick come to the Madang MAST in February as a volunteer team leader. It was a big job. At MAST events you must be prepared for anything, so he wasn't going to be able to wade into the water – he was going to have to go into the deep end first and we'd find out if he could swim.

Following the event, it was clear Patrick could be an asset to the team, but I wasn't convinced he was ready to run MAST for all of Papua New Guinea. While a good teacher and a solid Christian, there seemed to be gaps. It seemed that if I put him in a regional role, he would be able to have immediate impact on the team. Living in the Capital City, Port Moresby, and us not yet having a leader in the Southern region, I asked Patrick to take on that role. Of course, with One Tok, I had to explain why I didn't think it was appropriate for Patrick to lead the whole country, yet I still had a critical role for him.

At this point, Patrick has been involved in leading almost 10 training events, impacting dozens of languages in Papua New Guinea. He is developing his team in the southern region and developing

---

[45] Psalm 27:14

relationships with major church networks in the region, equipping their leaders so they can train language groups in the villages they serve.

The challenge of getting the Bible to every language in the next five years is one that requires significant capacity, particularly in places like Papua New Guinea where there are well over 1000 languages. This is a task that any one organization can not do on their own – it requires engagement of the worldwide Body of Christ. Patrick is one that is comfortable both in building his own team for the task and equipping other teams so they can work alongside his team.

The BATTLE Dream

Following the severing of the relationships with traditional Bible translation organizations in Papua New Guinea due to their rejection of MAST, Wycliffe Associates established a relationship with a small local non-profit organization. As Wycliffe Associates started becoming active in Bible translation in Papua New Guinea, through relationships with local churches, we quickly outgrew this small non-profit.

In December of 2018, we were having a prayer and planning summit in Papua New Guinea. The discussion was interesting, because the team was transparent in their wrestling with God. They were setting goals, and God was saying, "No, twice that." At twice that, the goals were scary – they were becoming God-sized goals.

Part of the discussion revolved around icare4U and alternatives. There was discussion about the national team forming their own association, focusing on literacy and Bible translation. Dan Kramer was in the meeting. Dan is the king of acronyms and can come up with an acronym for anything. Unfortunately, or perhaps fortunately, he jokingly suggested BATTLE – Bible Association for Translation, Teaching, and Literacy Education – and it stuck.

Chapter Eight

By July of 2019, all the government requirements to form the entity were completed, and we were ready to start the operations of BATTLE

Patrick has was involved in the formation of BATTLE. In July he was appointed Board President of BATTLE, while I serve alongside him as Vice President. While our desire is for BATTLE to be a nationally-controlled, nationally-run organization, in the initial formation, Wycliffe Associates is making two staff members available to serve on the Board to provide oversight as the organization is transitioning through its start-up phase.

For Patrick, this position on the Board is like my own position on the Wycliffe Associates Board where careful compartmentalization is needed. Patrick serves as a regional coordinator under Celsius. At the same time, he is part of the Board, that provides supervision of the executive director. So far, Patrick is doing a good job compartmentalizing between the roles.

It is interesting to see Patrick's compartmentalization between being a family member, being a member of the Board of BATTLE, and being a member of the operations team in the field, serving the church of Papua New Guinea. Serving the church is trumping family and the role on the Board.

> *"If anyone comes to me and does not hate his own father and mother and wife and children and brothers and sisters, yes, and even his own life, he cannot be my disciple.*[46]

Patrick is a disciple and makes life easier for Celsius and me with the southern region of Papua New Guinea under his watch. God is bringing us exactly everyone we need for the team.

---

[46] Luke 14:26

David

David is one of the newer leaders on the Papua New Guinea Team. I met him in March at the Great Commission Bible Translation Conference in Lae, but really didn't start to get to know him until after God gave me this book. David previously worked for a joint department between the Summer Institute of Linguistics and the Bible Translation Association of Papua New Guinea doing Church Engagement for Bible translation. He struggled with the strategy because his job was to cast vision for the churches to engage in Bible translation. This vision casting was being done at churches in the urban centers, yet the languages were in the villages. There was reluctance on the part of the department to engage in the villages because of the potential for violence. In his prior role, he was Assistant to the Director for Security at Ukarumpa and was getting pressure to bring a security firm in to supply guards for the facility. His suggestion that they needed more formal prayer was rebuffed. Here they were doing God's work but failing to depend on God.

David left the Summer Institute of Linguistics about seven years ago and relocated from the Highlands to New Britain Island to help with his wife's family's business. In early 2018, God pressed upon David's heart this scripture from the book of Isaiah.

> *Remember not the former things,*
> *nor consider the things of old.*
> *Behold, I am doing a new thing;*
> *now it springs forth, do you not perceive it?*
> *I will make a way in the wilderness*
> *and rivers in the desert.*
> *The wild beasts will honor me,*

> *the jackals and the ostriches,*
> *for I give water in the wilderness,*
> *rivers in the desert,*
> *to give drink to my chosen people,*
> *the people whom I formed for myself*
> *that they might declare my praise.*[47]

Kenneth had known David from the Highlands and his work with the Summer Institute of Linguistics. In March of this year Kenneth connected with David, and others went to New Britain to meet David and share with him about MAST. Understanding MAST, the scripture from Isaiah that God put on his heart that David and his wife had been praying about for the past year became clear. He knew of the old ways of Bible translation; and as he learned about MAST, he knew this was the new way God spoke of in Isaiah 43. David joined the team that month and is now using MAST to bring living water to the wilderness and fill rivers in the desert.

David is a seasoned pastor and filled with the Spirit. He is finding that God has prepared the way. God had impressed upon him the story of Nathanael.

> *Jesus saw Nathanael coming toward him and said of him, "Behold, an Israelite indeed, in whom there is no deceit!" Nathanael said to him, "How do you know me?" Jesus answered him, "Before Philip called you, when you were under the fig tree, I saw you."*[48]

David has had divine appointments where he is meeting people for the first time; and before he even introduces the topic of discussion, the people are asking if he is here to talk about Bible translation. Like Nathanael, God has shown them David, and they know David and

---

[47] Isaiah 43:18-21
[48] John 1:47-48

why God sent him. These individuals from various tribes are becoming the leaders of their language groups and driving the translation projects forward. Seeing this, David has adopted a strategy of praying over languages, asking God to prepare the meeting with the Nathanael from each the tribes.

An interesting thing has taken place with one of these groups. The language name stands for Bakovi or "I am a Man." The men have the final say, "This is my land, I will fight for the land, I will die for it." They are a culturally prideful clan. The men do men's work and don't get involved in the garden and other "non-manly work." The churches had very few men participating.

At the recent Kimbe, New Britain, event, this group had three women and one man as part of the translation team. As the scripture started coming to life in this language, men, particularly young men, started hearing the Word of God and coming to join the project. I received a recent report that less than two months after the initial training, the team is up to thirteen members and has translated and dedicated the four Gospels. This is nearly half the entire New Testament translated in less than two months. This living water has brought transformation of the church and community. These culturally prideful men are starting to follow Christ and coming to church. And this was one of the groups waiting for the expatriate experts when Celsius and the team showed up. The true experts were there within the tribe. They only found out when Celsius and the team told them who they really were, and God birthed His Word in their language through them.

He must increase, but I must decrease.[49]

This section has given you a glimpse into the team that God has called for leading this ministry in the two countries with the largest sections

---

[49] John 3:30

of the Pacific – Indonesia and Papua New Guinea. There is absolute commitment to the calling of God. There is also humility.

Recently Bruce Smith made a post on Facebook and reflects on a question he frequently ponders. "Why am I invited to participate in what God is doing in the world?" I ask this question "Why me?" of myself. I hear the same question from this team all the time. The question keeps us humble, as long as we keep walking in obedience and keep asking, "What next, God?"

Section Three

And let us consider how to stir up one another to love and good works, not neglecting to meet together, as is the habit of some, but encouraging one another, and all the more as you see the Day drawing near.[50]

---

[50] Hebrews 10:24-25 (ESV)

Chapter Nine – Sam and Steph

S am and Stephanie (Steph) are a young couple about my children's age. No nepotism at Wycliffe Associates, but I worked with Stephanie's father when he was serving as Chief Financial Officer and I was the Treasurer of Wycliffe Associates, and I regularly work with her mom in recruiting and Sam's mom in finance. I first met Sam in India in early 2016 – we were to co-lead an event, but instead, I got to fly off elsewhere and lead a small continuation event at my fourth event in any capacity. It would be two years before we overlapped in the field again.

In 2017 the Educational Services department was reorganized, and Sam became one of my managers. Wearing three hats in the organization, I had three different managers. Sam was clearly the youngest manager I had ever had, and certainly the biggest age gap; but the common vision made the age gap immaterial.

Reverse Mentor

Early on when reporting to Sam, he asked me to coach him as I saw coachable moments. I was one of several people both within Wycliffe Associates and outside that Sam had asked to provide him feedback.

I may have forgotten to tell Susan about this arrangement. Sam had a departmental gathering for training and prayer and the spouses were involved in the event. I was outside talking with Sam and Susan was within earshot. I was frank about some of my observations and prescriptive about what course of action I would take in Sam's situation.

Afterwards, Susan started asking me why I was doing that with Sam – to her it had seemed like I was insubordinate and telling him how to do his job. Within Wycliffe Associates, one of our core characteristics is humility. Sam had humbled himself and asked for the coaching help, recognizing that I'd been managing longer than he'd been breathing; and I held periodic conversations with him, in private (with no more than a spouse within earshot). I simply shared what I observed and how I might approach it. It was never, "You must do it this way"; it was always, "Here's what worked for me, for what it's worth." Susan was encouraged to hear I was mentoring Sam at his request and not being insubordinate.

It's Your Job

In the Pacific, we were gearing up for a leadership transition, where the present Regional MAST coordinator was moving on to a new role and he was raising up someone to replace him. The transition was long, over nearly a one-year period as the new person was raising support and Robert was training him.

As it was getting closer to the final transition, I started seeing evidence that the new coordinator just wasn't ready. Each time, I did some praying in my war room before I talked to Sam. I wanted to be supportive and not to have an appearance of impeding the transition. I was very content with my present roles, even though God had other intentions.

The first time was around Christmas of 2017. As I was praying and telling God I need to talk to Sam, God told me quite audibly, "It's your job." I said, "I know it's my job to talk to Sam." God said "No, it's your job." I felt like Jacob as he wrestled with God in Genesis 32. I didn't want the job. I enjoyed my present role, but there was no denying that God was telling me He anointed me for that role.

Over the coming months, leading to the transition in April of 2018, I had a number of conversations with God in the war room. It was always me praying and telling God I need to talk to Sam, then God telling me quite audibly, "It's your job." I would then acknowledge it's my job to talk to Sam. God would then reiterate, "No, it's your job." This was tough for me because I wanted to support the new person on the team, but God was clearly telling me it wasn't to be.

During that first week of the transition, I got a note when I was in Vanuatu that there had been a mistake and the person was being removed from the role. I found some time to talk to Sam, and he said he would find an interim person to fill the role until a permanent candidate was available.

The Pacific, like Asia, is very relational. We had a revolving door of leaders in the region over the past three years, and we were gearing up for another transition. I told Sam that an interim leader was a bad idea, particularly with some of the activity going on – it was likely to halt all momentum.

Sam processed my feedback and then asked if I would consider the role. I didn't have a choice – saying no would be disobedient to God, who had been preparing me for the anointing for over three months at that point. I told Sam I would pray on it. A few days later after talking with Susan, I told Sam the backstory of my wrestling with God and accepted the role.

Coming into a role like that with a clear divine anointing gives a certain boldness. Both knowing the region from working it for the previous two and a half years along with the anointing allowed me to get down to business quickly and start discerning His plans and tracking to them.

Sobbing

Several wives of colleagues have had some serious health problems that I've been regularly lifting up in prayer. Steph is one of them and has had a couple surgeries this year. With her problem not resolved, we were praying again during our gathering. I don't know exactly what Janet was praying for Steph at the moment, but I just started weeping in the Spirit. The weeping startled the rest of the group a bit – it was the first time Susan had truly heard it (hearing it through double pane windows from a barn in the next town doesn't count). The weeping brought joy to a tough situation, because the feelings of the Holy Spirit rose up and we were able to clearly see that as we grieved for Steph, the Holy Spirit did as well.

Change Agent

I had talked about God's anointing for the role and my conflict with the regional director with whom I had to work closely. Numerous times during that conflict either Dan Kramer or my wife Susan had to talk me off the ledge. Dan's big word was patience. My word was longsuffering. Susan kept reminding me of my calling. I had kept Sam out of the day-to-day of the conflict, interacting with his boss Dan, because of the politics involved. Both Dan and the other individual's manager reported directly to the VP of Operations.

During the time of prayer for each region during our MAST Regional Director offsite meeting in June of 2019, Steph had suggested that after prayer we have a time of reflection to see if God had a word for us.

So as the conflict was resolving, Sam received this word for me. It is as much for everything that had taken place in the Pacific, as well as what is ahead with the recent reorganization and my broader role in the Pacific.

Sam received a word for me and shared it. A few days later he sent me an email saying:

> *When we were praying for you, I said something along the lines of God knowing that the job was yours, not only for the work to be done but for the current situation that you're in. I want to reiterate that and express a little more. As I was praying these were the words that I received:*

"I set the table. You're where I put you for the work but also for the situation. This is your role but it's also your fight. Could you imagine if it was [your predecessor] in this situation with [him]? I know you want to remove yourself sometimes but all that would do is get rid of the piece (you) that I put on the board for this exact situation. The role that I told you was yours was bigger and different than you imagined. You are my change agent."

Dan recently shared in a meeting of the new Regional Directors about me being a "change agent." Dan said sometimes that is called a lightning rod.

Going where nobody has gone before tests the organization. Sometimes it causes strong negative reactions that can be like being hit with a bolt of lightning. Susan reminds me that God built me to have the courage to say what needs to be said and do what needs to be done, no matter the cost. I had a long legacy of this in my work in the secular world, telling my CEO and others what they needed to hear, which frequently wasn't what they wanted to hear.

God has given me stewardship over the team leading the area of the world with the greatest language density. Papua New Guinea, the Solomon Islands, and Vanuatu have the greatest language density per capita in the world. Indonesia has a mere thousand languages by the government's estimates. Beyond these challenges there are island nations and territories separated by thousands of miles of ocean from anyone else.

We can't keep doing Bible translation like it's been done in the Pacific since the 1950s, perhaps earlier. The job has not been getting done.

Joy at Home

In September of 2019, I was coming to Orlando for a couple days for some meetings related to an Operations reorganization. I asked Sam if I could take him up on his offer to stay at his home. I got a conditional yes – I could stay, but they'd appreciate some help from me with some prayer to deal with some unwelcome spiritual guests that had been left behind by some roommates.

We talked through the situation, and it seemed that these unwelcome guests were specifically permitted by Steph to stay in a specific area of the house – like the guest room I was using. As we talked through it, I suggested we have a time of repentance and then a time of worship. We did and I recall a bit of weeping in the Spirit as we repented. We then moved on to intercession and worship. After that time of communion with the Lord, it felt like it was time to move over to the affected area of the house. Steph led the prayer, with Sam and me supporting. The Spirit was definitely guiding my prayer and had me weeping in the Spirit. It was powerful and we knew we had achieved victory over darkness and the prayer transitioned to thanksgiving. As we moved to thanksgiving, I remember us playing *Raise a Hallelujah* by Bethel.

The next day, Steph told me she felt joy was back in the home – that the darkness was gone. This simple process of adoring God, confession, thanksgiving, and supplication returned joy to their home.

> *Above all, keep loving one another earnestly, since love covers a multitude of sins. Show hospitality to one another without grumbling. As each has received a gift, use it to serve one another, as good stewards of God's varied grace.*[51]

Sam and Stephanie are one couple that Susan and I have been able to love on and be loved back. We have different gifts. Sometimes our gifts have been a blessing to them, at other times, their gifts have been a blessing to us. I believe all of us have grown through the relationship.

---

[51] 1 Peter 4:8-10

Chapter Ten – Shakil

S hakil is a divine friend. I say that in the truest sense of the word. God has woven us together and there is no human reason for the depth of the friendship – it is all God. Paul's letter to the Philippians starts with *Paul and Timothy, servants of Christ Jesus.*[52] That is the glue between Shakil and me, we have this Paul-Timothy relationship, and the yoke that ties us together is our mutual surrender to serve Christ Jesus to bring scripture to the ends of the earth. It has been a blessing to be used by God to answer Shakil's prayer for reengagement in the ministry of Bible translation.

I was first introduced to Shakil by email in July of 2017 when I took on the role of MAST Coordinator for South Asia. Shakil had been talking with Dan Kramer and was a good lead to help us start MAST in Bangladesh. He was born in Bangladesh to a Muslim family. He accepted Christ and for a period worked for a local Bible translation organization in Bangladesh, but left hungering for the church to have an active role in Bible translation.

We spoke recently about this calling for Bible translation. While working promoting Bible translation in Bangladesh from 2007 to 2013, Shakil was responsible for mobilizing the Bangladesh church for Bible translation but saw zero new Bible translation projects in the country. The barriers to entry to raise someone up to participate in Bible translation took too long as there was much education needed to meet the criteria to be a translator with traditional Bible translation organizations.

---

[52] Philippians 1:1

Shakil's frustration grew the longer he worked with the western controlled Bible translation organization, with more time spent in meetings and conferences talking about the well-understood need to involve the church in Bible translation but little time focused on solutions to get church involvement. There was also lots of discussion on how to engage the church once scripture was completed. All during this time, people continued to die without hearing God's Word in their heart language.

> But understand this, that in the last days there will come times of
> difficulty. People … having the appearance of godliness,
> but denying its power. … always learning and never able to arrive
> at a knowledge of the truth.[53]

The Pahan language translation was a 40-year project. Because the Pahan population wasn't "large enough," five "closely related" languages were merged together into a single Bible. This wasn't a scripture engagement problem – this was a Bible quality problem – the Bible was rejected by the church because it wasn't any one of the five languages it was targeted to address – it was bits and pieces of each of those five languages, and it didn't make sense to any of them. Unfortunately, with the outsourced model of Bible translation, where foreigners do their best to learn the language and do the translation, anecdotal evidence suggests this creation of Bibles in invented languages that nobody speaks happens quite frequently.

In 2013 Jewan, a national Bible translation partner in Nepal was talking to Dan Kramer about the need for a methodology for the local church to do Bible translation. At the same time Shakil left the local Bible translation organization and immigrated to the US. He was discouraged, because he saw great barriers to this happening in the

---

[53] 2 Timothy 3:1,5,7

traditional Bible translation organizations. Shakil kept praying that God would raise up someone to bring Bible translation to the church.

Two years later, one of his colleagues in Bangladesh had heard about MAST, but also heard the propaganda about it being too fast. He shared with Shakil about it and Shakil felt God had answered his prayer.

With my roles running MAST in South Asia and the Gateway Language Program, our first face-to-face meeting was many months after Dan's introduction, February of 2018. I made a day trip to Detroit where Shakil had a thriving ministry to the Muslim community and a growing church plant.

We had lunch at Shakil's home and I shocked his wife Angela with my action at the lunch she prepared. In South Asia it is common practice to eat with your fingers rather than utensils. She had prepared a wonderful South Asian meal. As it was being served, she offered me utensils, while everyone else was using fingers. Given my many trips to India in the previous two years, I was comfortable eating as they do in South Asia, so I refused the utensils.

Throughout 2018, Shakil and I continued to build the relationship, with me looking for opportunities to help him get some MAST experience under his belt and to figure out the best fit for him within Wycliffe Associates.

In November of 2018, I lined Shakil up to join our Indonesian team for a two-week MAST event in Jayapura, Papua, Indonesia. I had just finished time in Papua and was going home. We met briefly in the Jakarta airport, as I was heading home, and Chuck and Shakil were coming in to Indonesia for two different events. I was slated to be back in less than two weeks and had a couple of days between meetings in Indonesia and Papua New Guinea, so Shakil and I made plans to get together in Jakarta after his MAST event.

In our first day in Jakarta, we were having a coffee and Shakil said, "I want to carry your bag." I started to say you're saying this without understanding all that is on my plate. He quickly interrupted and told me in Bangla culture, carrying someone's bag is a deep commitment – Shakil was saying that he was fully committed to me no matter the cost. Whenever, whatever, however – he would be there. It is a covenant up there with the marriage covenant Susan and I share.

As our relationship is developing, in some sense it is a Paul-Timothy relationship. Shakil is a generation younger than me, and recently lost his father after an unexpected illness.

> *With the offer to carry my bag, it still wasn't clear how best to utilize Shakil. He is a networker and mobilizer with extensive global connections. I was with him in Orlando in February of 2019 and made a side comment about Fiji. Within minutes he had me talking on the phone with a pastor friend of his in Fiji who had gone to the Youth with a Mission (YWAM) Discipleship Training School (DTS) with him in Thailand.*

In March of 2019 we were together in Papua New Guinea for a Great Commission Bible Translation Conference. Here, one of his friends from DTS lived in the area and came in to see him. Not only did this friend know Shakil, the friend was well connected to a number of members of the Papua New Guinea team, including Misson. Small world.

Back to the Pahan people. Earlier this year, Shakil was able to take MAST to Bangladesh for the first time. Pahan was one of the language groups that Shakil and the team empowered to translate God's Word into their heart language. As one who was raised with scripture in my native tongue, it is hard to imagine the separation that happens when you don't have God's Word in your mother tongue and then the great joy when you finally feel part of the Kingdom with His Word in your language. God becomes bigger when He speaks your language.

Sometime after the training event Shakil visited three of the villages where Pahan is spoken. He and his team were given a royal welcome. The people are very poor,[54] but they welcomed Shakil with their best. As part of the welcome, they washed his feet first in water and dried with a new towel, then with milk. Shakil doesn't deserve this type of honor – none of us do; however, sometimes we need to allow others the gift of blessing us, even if it makes us uncomfortable. This is a lesson Celsius has been teaching me. Shakil is just a vessel of the global MAST team, just like the rest of us, but to many of these communities that have been denied scripture for decades, like the Ontenu, like the Sawi, and like the Pahan, we have the privilege of bringing God to life for these people so they hear Him speak their language. Furthermore, there is more self-worth, because these people are equipped to do translation themselves and to sustain God's Word and without depending on someone from the outside.

As we move into this next season in the Pacific, Shakil will be working alongside me, working to open the doors in the 20 countries and territories remaining for Wycliffe Associates to begin work in the Pacific. With his calling, his passion, his MAST experience, and networking ability, I expect he will quickly locate the doors God needs us to open.

This season will not be easy. Paul charges Timothy to *"wage the good warfare, holding faith and a good conscience."*[55] Recently Shakil met with an old friend of his father's to talk about Bible translation. It was a very

---

[54] In many locations in the global south where Wycliffe Associates serves the church, communities practice substance living, raising their own food and living very simply. They don't have money or other assets we'd see in the western world.

[55] 1 Timothy 1:18

difficult meeting. Shakil had to listen to the man that Shakil had a lifetime of respect for berate him and refer to Wycliffe Associates as a cult. Following two hours of respectful listening, Shakil asked the man some questions.

> *Beloved, do not believe every spirit, but test the spirits to see whether they are from God, for many false prophets have gone out into the world. By this you know the Spirit of God: every spirit that confesses that Jesus Christ has come in the flesh is from God.*[56]

The Bible tells us the impact of scripture. The Bible is a way toward understanding salvation.[57] Shakil asked if through the Bible translation projects where he had been involved, did he see people coming to faith. The man had not. Shakil shared how he has baptized Muslims, Hindus, and Buddhists who have participated in MAST projects.

The Bible revives the soul.[58] Shakil asked the man if he had seen any sense of revival in the community or individuals from scripture translation? Again, the response was no. Shakil then shared about church plants he has seen following the initiation of MAST projects.

Shakil continued with several measures that we have in what we call the Biblical outcomes rubric – truths from scripture about the transformative effect of scripture on people's lives.

> *And the Lord's servant must not be quarrelsome but kind to everyone, able to teach, patiently enduring evil, correcting his opponents with gentleness. God may perhaps grant them repentance leading to a knowledge of the truth, and they may come*

---

[56] 1 John 4:1-2
[57] 2 Peter 3:15-16
[58] Psalms 19:7-11

*to their senses and escape from the snare of the devil, after being
captured by him to do his will.*[59]

These are not unique things that only Shakil has experienced. Every
one of us involved in MAST has seen these changes. Prisoners
translating a New Testament in mere weeks and gaining hope through
the process. The Bible is instruction to give hope.[60] Did Paul have hope
in prison? Shouldn't God's Word bring hope to prisoners today
through Bible translation?

MAST is misunderstood by many individuals involved in other
methods of Bible translation. Can we deny the quality of scripture
produced through MAST when the evidence of biblical transformation
is overwhelming? We're told in John 14 that the part of the role of the
Holy Spirit is to teach us all things and remind us of everything Jesus
said. To me that sounds like the Holy Spirit was entrusted by God with
Bible translation quality. Since it is also the Holy Spirit that brings
people to faith, it is the Holy Spirit that is using Scripture translated in
the Spirit using the MAST methodology to bring people to faith. Based
on the results, it seems the Holy Spirit is affirming the MAST
methodology.

I am blessed to have Shakil as part of the team. He loves me and prays
consistently for me. He encourages me. I don't need yes-men on the
team; but I do need people beside me in the spiritual battle, like Susan
and Shakil that can keep me focused on the truth and focused on the
big picture so that we get to make a difference. We get the opportunity
to bring languages from the status of not having a verse of scripture to
having some scripture. Last year we saw nearly 200 languages make
that transition in the Pacific. If we succeed in God's plan, we will see
on average three to four Pacific languages a day get some scripture for

---

[59] 2 Timothy 2:24-26
[60] Romans 15:4, Psalms 119:9

_the first time in 2020, with church ownership to follow through to the completion of their Bibles.

Pray for Shakil and me as we work through Australia, Micronesia, and Polynesia to raise up the churches to bring God's Word to their tribal languages. Pray 1 Timothy 1:18-19 for us to wage the good warfare, holding faith and a good conscience. We will face great opposition, but the opposition isn't rooted in the people, particularly those involved in traditional Bible translation; the opposition is rooted in the Evil One, who doesn't want the truth brought to light.

the first time in 2020, with church ownership to follow through to the completion of their Bibles.

Pray for Shakil and me as we work through Australia, Micronesia, and Polynesia to raise up the churches to bring God's Word to their tribal languages. Pray 1 Timothy 1:18-19 for us to wage the good warfare, holding faith and a good conscience. We will face great opposition, but the opposition isn't rooted in the people, particularly those involved in traditional Bible translation; the opposition is rooted in the Evil One, who doesn't want the truth brought to light.

Section Four

For we must all appear before the judgment seat of Christ, so that each one may receive what is due for what he has done in the body, whether good or evil.[61]

Chapter Eleven – My Best Friend

For God will never give you the spirit of fear, but the Holy Spirit who gives you mighty power, love, and self-control.[62]

A s Christians, we all want a close personal relationship with Jesus Christ. Jesus left us. He left us for a reason. He left us so that the Holy Spirit could come and could be a part of us. For many Christians, we focus on two of the three parts of the trinity, and don't give the Holy Spirit the same attention. John records the words of Jesus,

"And I will ask the Father, and he will give you another Helper, to be with you forever, even the Spirit of truth, whom the world cannot receive, because it neither sees him nor knows him. You know him, for he dwells with you and will be in you."[63]

He is our advocate. He is our intercessor. And He can be grieved deeply.

Steps of Faith

As I reflect, God has had me on a walk of blind obedience until I grew to a point of being able to clearly see in both the light and the darkness. Most Americans do not acknowledge the realm of darkness surrounding us around the world. This is Satan's kingdom that we are living in, and God wants our obedience to fulfill His purpose. That is

---

[62] 2 Tim 1:7 (TPT)
[63] John 14:16-17

why we are called to be in this world and not of this world. Careful reading of scripture shows us that we must keep our faith. The enemy is always on the prowl for us.

In 2006 Susan wanted us to get baptized before we were married to be born again and show that the blood of Jesus has washed away all that sin. I followed. Each of us were baptized as infants in a Roman Catholic church, but neither had made our own personal public profession of faith. The baptism was her idea, and I was good with it, but I wouldn't say I was sold out on it. God has been faithful, despite my being lukewarm at the time of my baptism. He called me forward and continues to call me forward today. I'm convinced that a big part of this grace is dying to self and serving with humility and obedience.

> *But he gives more grace. Therefore it says, "God opposes the proud but gives grace to the humble." Submit yourselves therefore to God. Resist the devil, and he will flee from you. Draw near to God and he will draw near to you. Cleanse your hands, you sinners, and purify your hearts, you double-minded. Be wretched and mourn and weep.*[64]

If you haven't figured it out yet, I'm just a ragamuffin, a sinner, a fallen man. I'd say God uses me in spite of my flaws, but the truth is, most days He uses me because of all my flaws.

The step of moving to Vermont was one of faith – that God was asking us to serve the widow, but we had no idea how God really intended to use that step. Moving to Vermont to care for Susan's mom prepared us for full-time ministry. We sold our home which retired the large mortgage and eventually I was released from the secular job that was holding us back from serving full time in ministry. Many Christians serve God well in the secular world. With the role I'm now in, clearly

---

[64] James 4:6-9

God built me for this season, and I would have missed it if we had not stepped out in faith.

The sabbatical was a second big step of faith – this was dipping the toes into full-time ministry without burning the boats. After 12 months I could have gone back to secular employment and this would have been a nice little recharge. Now, I can never go back – the only thing that will stop me in finishing this work is my own martyrdom.

Susan was frustrated when she couldn't carry me through the trial I went through this year that I described in the beginning of section two. In the middle of the refiner's fire earlier this year, I was ready to throw in the towel. Satan had a pretty big hold on me, casting much doubt and discouragement, but many people prayed me through it, and I came out the other end forged for this new season of significant acceleration of pace.

First Memories – Lake Mendocino

I spoke of my journey to discover the hurts I had caused my older son. As I was sitting around the campfire, I just got this feeling of wanting to crawl out of my skin, that what the teens were sharing was what my son could not vocalize. The Holy Spirit was helping me see that this was me. I got the courage to speak, to confess to this circle of 100 people that what I was hearing was what I was doing, and yet, I was the sober one in the household. It was a humbling experience, but a crucial one in breaking that multigenerational legacy of emotional abuse. It also was step of obedience in following the prompting of the Spirit even though I was not comfortable following that prompt. This would be one of several occasions where I saw myself as the older son from the Parable of the Prodigal Son.[65] I justified my actions because I was the

---

[65] Luke 15:11-32

more functional parent, yet I had my own sin and shortcomings that I was justifying and ignoring.

First Words

Part of our journey as a Christian is to develop our relationship with God so that we are able to hear Him and trust in the Holy Spirit. What good is prayer if we don't actually listen? My first mountain-top experience where there was no doubt in conversing and hearing God was in Thailand. I was leading a MAST workshop where the team was translating the Mandarin New Testament as part of the Mandarin Gateway Language Project.

During the workshop, I dined each night with groups of translators. During one dinner, I shared a story of God's redemption of translators working with us from the Middle East. These translators were former terrorists with some of the well-known terrorist groups in the Middle East. During the start of one event, some staff from Wycliffe Associates prayed for these former terrorists, now Bible translators. One by one they fell prostrate as hands were laid on them. About 40 minutes later when one of them came to, he was asked what happened. He said that as he was prayed over, he saw this bright white light, whiter than anything he had ever seen. Out of this light emerged Jesus. Jesus then spoke to him, and told him for every life he took, he would now bring a hundred-fold to the kingdom. After I shared this story, one of the young translators wanted to speak to me.

We spoke the following day, and it was pretty clear this young man was tormented by some demons. I had never dealt with this before, but through other spiritual warfare battles I faced, I started reading up on the topic and had read Karl Payne's book *Spiritual Warfare* (Payne, 2011), which was very prescriptive about doing deliverances.

Chapter Eleven

I had been conversing back and forth with our Chaplain at Wycliffe Associates and we agreed a period of prayer and fasting both in Asia and America would be a good preparatory step.

I spoke with the young man. I would classify him as a nominal Christian at the time. He identified as a Christian, but many parts of his life were not surrendered to Christ. He desired to be delivered from the torment and eagerly took on the homework. In preparation I asked him to review Galatians 5:19-21, Mark 7:21-23, and Colossians 3:5-8 and write down any areas in these passages that are habitual problems. I also asked him to share his struggles with his translation team, who were peers from where he lived. He needed accountability and support afterwards, something I couldn't provide living half a world away.

I had planned to do the deliverance the evening following a 24-hour fast. Around lunchtime I felt this urging that it should be done then. I remember two walking prayers as I was gathering the team. "God, make me ready for this" and "God, fill me with the Holy Spirit." I immediately got two-word responses to each of the two requests. "You're ready," followed by "You're filled."

While I facilitated the process, it was his willingness during the deliverance that ensured success. I have had others where Christians have not been willing to confess all their sins, and therefore, footholds still existed. He demonstrated willingness to confess all his sins that provided a foothold, to ask God to cancel all ground given over to the demons, and to command the demons to leave. This final point is anchored on the authority, victory, protection, and position that was purchased at Calvary by the death, resurrection, and intercession of Jesus Christ, and delegated to every Christian.

The deliverance process went very smoothly, to the point that afterwards, one of our expat facilitators asked me how many times I had done a deliverance, to which I responded, "Only this one."

Blessed is the man who trusts in the Lord, whose trust is the Lord. He is like a tree planted by water, that sends out its roots by the stream, and does not fear when heat comes, for its leaves remain green,
and is not anxious in the year of drought, for it does not cease to bear fruit.[66]

Embracing All of Him

Over the past four years, I've had numerous encounters with the Holy Spirit at different events and, lately, more and more back on US soil. This has included prophetic words, visions and dreams, the ministry of healing, and the gift of faith. Overseas, we are in a dark environment with obvious spiritual warfare, so we and our prayer partners pray us up for it, and we're tuned in to the Spirit, therefore we see more active gifting from the Spirit. At home, I can get complacent, and the intimacy with the Spirit and gifting isn't as strong.

At an event in West Africa in 2016, one of our development directors prayed us through a prayer from 2 Corinthians 10:2-6.

I beg of you that when I am present I may not have to show boldness with such confidence as I count on showing against some who suspect us of walking according to the flesh. For though we walk in the flesh, we are not waging war according to the flesh. For the weapons of our warfare are not of the flesh but have divine power to destroy strongholds. We destroy arguments and every lofty opinion raised against the knowledge of God, and take every thought captive to obey Christ, being ready to punish every disobedience, when your obedience is complete.[67]

---

[66] Jeremiah 17:7-8
[67] 2 Corinthians 10:2-6

Chapter Eleven

The battles we face, although they may sometimes appear to be human conflict are not of the flesh. This awareness that the spiritual warfare is a continuous part of what we do, and everything we do has an earthly component and a heavenly component, has drawn me closer to God and to the trinity. No longer is the Holy Spirit just a vapor or spirit. He is an integral part of me, and we've developed such a bond that He has blessed me with something I never would have chosen on my own, the gift of weeping in the Spirit. So often someone will be praying (even my own prayers), and something in that prayer will be something that grieves the Holy Spirit and I get to weep with Him. It's shocked people alongside me when they haven't been aware of this gift. It's not a normal human weeping.

At the Indonesian Prayer Summit that just ended, I laid hands on one of my Papuan brothers to pray on him following John's anointing. Immediately upon laying hands I wept. This man is a marked man. He has been arrested and dragged off for questioning by police and military because he is believed to be part of the independence movement within Papua. Papuan church leaders are pleading for us to pray and appeal to the United Nations. In that moment of weeping and the subsequent prayers for him and the rest of the Papuan team, we all knew that the Holy Spirit is grieved by this situation.

Reading the Bible has helped me some, but last year I stepped up the game after Susan suggested we do the Tim Challies Christian Reading Challenge (Challies, 2018). With a crazy year of travel, I had lots of opportunity to read and read 74 books, including my annual cover-to-cover read of the Bible. This year I've repeated the challenge and have read over 100 books so far, with few days left to go this year. Tim challenges you to read a wide variety of both Christian and secular books. Both years I've done a bit of reading on prayer and on spiritual warfare. This summer it seemed I needed to do a crash course on operating in the Glory zone and on the Holy Spirit.

*And he gave the apostles, the prophets, the evangelists, the
shepherds and teachers, to equip the saints for the work of ministry,
for building up the body of Christ, until we all attain to the unity
of the faith and of the knowledge of the Son of God, to mature
manhood, to the measure of the stature of the fullness of Christ, so
that we may no longer be children, tossed to and fro by the waves
and carried about by every wind of doctrine, by human cunning, by
craftiness in deceitful schemes. Rather, speaking the truth in love,
we are to grow up in every way into him who is the head, into
Christ, from whom the whole body, joined and held together by
every joint with which it is equipped, when each part is working
properly, makes the body grow so that it builds itself up in love.*[68]

I do not think this growth in the Spirit these recent months was solely
for my benefit. The bigger the national team gets, the further I am from
the front lines of the battle. I feel a strong calling that my preparation
was not only for my benefit, also it was for building up the national
team.

This calling was recently confirmed with a prophecy that was given to
a pastor that I've met who is connected to Celsius. I started my crash
course on the Glory zone (where heaven descends to earth and opens
and we can operate in the Spirit in the heavenlies) and the Holy Spirit,
on August 8th, with those studies continuing through September. Just
over a week later, on August 17th Pastor Siki had a vivid dream. It was
so intense that he journaled it. A week or two before my most recent
trip to Papua New Guinea he shared with Celsius, and God started
repeating the dream, clarifying it further. Pastor Siki has sensed a
calling to establish a house of healing and sees the SUN Literacy
program as part of that – allowing the deaf to hear God's Word and the
deaf-blind to see God's Word.

---

[68] Ephesians 4:11-16

In the dream Pastor Siki shared with Celsius, I was at the gate at this large house, and the house had a tank with exceedingly pure olive oil. Celsius was in the house. The interpreters of the dream explained that I was the anointed gatekeeper. The oil was provided for three purposes – for anointing of people, for healing, and for infilling of the Holy Spirit. I see evidence of God calling me for each of these purposes. The work Celsius and I, along with the rest of the team are being called to do will heal people, but more importantly will heal nations. Celsius had a prophetic word given to him that he would meet with leaders and high government officials. We haven't seen that yet, but can see God moving Celsius in that direction. I believe God is calling for more direct usage of the oil of infilling. God has used me to heal Kenneth's relationship with the Holy Spirit; and with the Prayer Summit, a goal was to strengthen the entire team's relationship, baptizing them in the Spirit if they are not already baptized in the Spirit.

When we look at the different purposes of the oil in this prophecy, it is all biblical. There are many passages in the Bible on anointing of people.

> *But when you fast, anoint your head and wash your face, that your fasting may not be seen by others but by your Father who is in secret. And your Father who sees in secret will reward you.*[69]

> *You shall anoint Aaron and his sons, and consecrate them, that they may serve me as priests. And you shall say to the people of Israel, 'This shall be my holy anointing oil throughout your generations.*[70]

We also see the use of oil for the ministry of healing.

---

[69] Matthew 6:17-18
[70] Exodus 30:30-31

Is anyone among you sick? Let him call for the elders of the church, and let them pray over him, anointing him with oil in the name of the Lord. And the prayer of faith will save the one who is sick, and the Lord will raise him up. And if he has committed sins, he will be forgiven. Therefore, confess your sins to one another and pray for one another, that you may be healed.[71]

Finally, we see the use of oil in the infilling of the Spirit.

And the Lord said, "Arise, anoint him, for this is he." 13 Then Samuel took the horn of oil and anointed him in the midst of his brothers. And the Spirit of the Lord rushed upon David from that day forward. And Samuel rose up and went to Ramah.[72]

This anointing by the Lord for the task of discipling the churches of the Pacific is being seen in many ways. Not only in dreams and visions, not only in words given to me directly or given through others, but also in visual manifestations. I have had people both in America and in the Pacific that are highly tuned to the Spirit comment that when I am leading prayer or sharing about this work of God, they see a yarmulke on my head – the traditional Jewish skull cap. I'm not of Jewish descent that I know of, but the vision is just another manifestation of the anointing – an anointing that is only through God's almighty grace and solely for His glory.

Thus says the Lord of hosts: In those days ten men from the nations of every tongue shall take hold of the robe of a Jew, saying, let us go with you, for we have heard that God is with you.[73]

I'm still a ragamuffin, but God has drawn me to him and prepared me for today. The intimacy with the Holy Spirit can be overwhelming at

---

[71] James 5:14-16
[72] 1 Samuel 16:12b-13
[73] Zechariah 8:23

times, but shouldn't all our encounters with God be overwhelming? I'm so grateful for this intimacy, because I know I don't face these battles alone. God is with me.

This war is real. Around the world, we have translators killed on a pretty regular basis. One of the countries I serve has the world's largest Islamic population. In many of the other countries I serve, witchcraft is still common and cannibalism isn't a distant memory but a memory in their lifetime. One of our translators has transitioned from headhunter to soul hunter – he carries his Bible in his bilum where he used to carry body parts of those he'd killed. I don't doubt that members of my team will be martyred. I may be martyred myself, but it is worth the price.

I remember receiving a note from Bruce in 2016 about a terrorist attack on a team's translation office. Two men were killed by gunfire. Two of the men ran upstairs and shielded the leader with their bodies. These two men were beaten to death by the terrorists with their now empty rifles. The leader survived and wrote Wycliffe Associates to say that the translations were safe. His comment to us, "Hang in there – it's worth it."

That said, operating in the Spirit, we are more likely to stay in the center of God's will in these battles. That doesn't guarantee our safety, but operating outside His will certainly doesn't guarantee our safety. I don't want to be Balaam.

> *Then the Lord opened the eyes of Balaam, and he saw the angel of the Lord standing in the way, with his drawn sword in his hand. And he bowed down and fell on his face. And the angel of the Lord said to him, "Why have you struck your donkey these three times? Behold, I have come out to oppose you because your way is perverse before me. The donkey saw me and turned aside before me these*

three times. If she had not turned aside from me, surely just now I would have killed you and let her live.[74]

---

[74] Numbers 22:31-33

Chapter Twelve – Finishing Vision 2025

Shepherd the flock of God that is among you, exercising oversight, not under compulsion, but willingly, as God would have you; not for shameful gain, but eagerly; not domineering over those in your charge, but being examples to the flock. And when the chief Shepherd appears, you will receive the unfading crown of glory.[75]

There is a book, *Eye to Eye, Heart to Heart,* (Crough & Crough, 2007) that is readily available in the Wycliffe Associates offices and in the Wycliffe Apartments that was published a dozen years ago. This book contains a section talking about Vision 2025, the history of the development of the vision by John Watters, then incoming Executive Director of Wycliffe International (now the Wycliffe Global Alliance).

Eye to Eye, Heart to Heart says that Vision 2025 stands on five pillars or themes:

1. Urgency
2. Partnership
3. Capacity Building
4. Creative Strategies
5. Sustainability

---

[75] 1 Peter 5:2-4

I've been in many discussions about the desire for reconciliation and collaboration between Wycliffe Associates and other long time Bible translation and linguistics organizations. While a laudable goal, in my opinion, the organizations currently have different missions and different core principles. I remember one retired executive sharing with me the importance of not losing our mission.

It is my opinion that Vision 2025 is not a statement developed by man, but rather a mandate from God. The more we operate with childlike faith, the greater miracles and capacity building we see in the efforts of Bible translation using MAST. It can only be of God. Brent Ropp recently shared with me that he clearly remembers two points a speaker made about Vision 2025 at a meeting of Bible translation organizations in 2004. The speaker said Vision 2025 will happen only if God desires it and only if the worldwide Church partners in it.

As I've synthesized where God is leading me, the team in the Pacific, and Wycliffe Associates, He has raised us up to be shepherds to disciple the Body of Christ to be the stewards of God's Word in their heart language. They have the responsibility and the authority to steward the Word of God. And this task is the mandate or commandment we got from Jesus – the Great Commission.

> *Then Jesus came to them and said, "All authority in heaven and on earth has been given to me. Therefore go and make disciples of all nations, baptizing them in the name of the Father and of the Son and of the Holy Spirit, and teaching them to obey everything I have commanded you. And surely I am with you always, to the very end of the age."*[76]

Fundamentally, I believe Wycliffe Associates is teaching the church how to fish with respect to Bible translation – giving them the

---

[76] Matthew 28:18-20

methodology, training, and tools to steward the Word of God in their language. Other translation organizations want the church engaged but believe external consultants are required to clean the fish, and as such are fundamentally providing the fish, rather than teaching how to fish. In many cases, the fish is either spoiled when it is delivered to the church or after some time, spoils, with nobody trained to catch and clean another fish.

As I look at the five themes, personally I see only Wycliffe Associates and our partners dying to self and surrendering all to align with these five pillars. We see the urgency and have deeply committed to see the vision fulfilled. April 2018 – April 2019 was a period where I was away from home 80 percent of the time, most of that time without my wife with me. It was not easy, but it was necessary. With the growing strength of the Pacific team, that period of discipleship of the team was a great investment.

Urgency – The finish line of Vision 2025 is a mere five years away, which means honestly only two to three years to start the last language if we are to have complete Bibles by 2025. While the mandate is one thing, the other part is souls keep dying without the task being done.

I was in Madang in February and heard a man tell me the story about his father making trips in 2012 and 2013 to plead with other Bible translation organizations operating in Papua New Guinea, and being refused both times. In 2014 on his death bed, he urged his sons to never give up trying to get scripture for his people. Unfortunately, I've also heard stories of Wycliffe Associates dropping the ball in the early days of MAST. We weren't prepared for the demand and didn't yet have the necessary management systems in place. Now we're at the next transition – getting out of the way altogether, so as churches disciple each other, there is no dependency on Wycliffe Associates.

Whether you talk to Bruce Smith, Tim Neu, Brent Ropp, Dan Kramer, myself, Celsius, Kenneth, Christov, Shakil – every one of us is committed to ensuring quality scripture is in the hands of the language groups as quickly as possible so we don't have to see another soul die without having heard God in their heart language. That is the urgency driving us just as hard as the God-sized calling of Vision 2025 – Our brothers and sisters that don't have the same opportunity as we do to hear God in their heart language. It isn't a competition, it is a compulsion to finish the task.

Partnership – As stated at least fifteen years ago, this Vision only happens if the global church carries the work forward. Wycliffe Associates can't possibly build the capacity, but the global church can and is building this capacity and translating God's Word at unprecedented speed.

Capacity building – Again, it is the global church that will provide the capacity. We see with simple discipleship, multiplication can quickly happen. Jesus taught us how to disciple and multiply.

Creative Strategies – Working for and with Dan Kramer is a joy. He is always both looking for innovation and encouraging us to innovate. MAST is an innovation and gift from God to quickly equip local churches for Bible translation. MAST equips the church to do quality checking. With traditional translation, there is a requirement for external checking of translated scripture, and there is a shortage of consultants to do the checking. The delay between translation of scripture and consultant checking is frequently measured in years. It is like catching a fish and waiting years before cleaning it. People starve to death before being able to be fed the Word of God. Furthermore, the requirement of external consultant checking creates a dependency that is a barrier to full stewardship by the local church.

Chapter Twelve

Bruce Smith, when he visited the Sawi in January of 2019, asked the church leaders two questions. The first was "What makes you think you are qualified to translate the Bible into Sawi?" Their response was "We have been a witness to our neighbors near and far. ... We have the Holy Spirit to teach and correct us. Only a person who doesn't know us would ask this question. If we are not qualified to translate the Bible in our own language, then no one is." Bruce went on to ask them what they would say if someone came to ask about checking the translation. Each of the leaders had the same response: "Do they speak Sawi?" (Smith, 2020).

Many innovations have been done on top of MAST, and God has provided tools for the deaf, deaf illiterate, and deaf-blind. We are testing an offshoot from SUN that could produce a New Testament for the blind that is under three hundred pages – just a page per chapter. Today the blind can't bring their braille Bible to church or a Bible study, because it takes an entire floor-to-ceiling bookcase. We need to keep working with partners and innovating to have the proper tools for every situation to be encountered.

Sustainability – If the language owns the translation and has the tools to do the translation, they also own the ability to maintain the work and to do derivative works, including study Bibles, children's Bibles, or audio Bibles. I've got several national staff members that are very vocal that the local church has outsourced stewardship of God's Word, and this outsourcing practice needs to stop immediately. Other translation organizations believe outside consultants are the best stewards of the language of the local Body of Christ and have convinced the Body of Christ that Bible translation must be outsourced. With translations requiring the approval of outsiders, the local Body of Christ can never achieve a state of self-sufficiency. The point is not training the church so they can just have a translation, but rather training so they can sustain forever.

Today, language groups aren't solely dependent on Wycliffe Associates for training in MAST – we train every language group so they can train their neighbors. The apostles weren't the only ones to disciple. They discipled to make disciples who then discipled others. The ultimate goal is that stewardship of God's Word is returned to the local church. Everything we do is to equip and empower the church for that stewardship responsibility. In 2016 when he was interviewed by Missions News Network on Wycliffe Associates' withdrawal from the Wycliffe Global Alliance, Bruce Smith said "The local Body of Christ has both the responsibility and authority as stewards of God's Word in their language."[77] In Bruce's book *Living Translation: Peace Children* (Smith, 2020), he states: "We may not have realized that God has been preparing His Church, the local language experts, to steward his Word for their own people."

Some would say we are delusional to think we can see Vision 2025 fulfilled with just five years left and thousands of languages remaining. As Christov's former managing partner said, "I cannot counteroffer God." We see God's fingerprints all over the work in the Pacific and we see hundreds of languages just desperate for the Word of God and ready to resume their stewardship of their languages. Madang Province was one of the first places I clearly saw that mighty rushing wind, but it is sweeping across both the Papua and Papua New Guinea sides of New Guinea Island.

> *But Jesus looked at them and said, "With man this is impossible, but with God all things are possible."*[78]

In the five-year history of the MAST methodology, the many scriptureless language communities and churches longing for God's

[77] https://www.mnnonline.org/news/wycliffe-associates-departing-from-wycliffe-global-alliance/
[78] Matthew 19:26

Word in their heart language have been consistent proponents. They want to catch and clean their own fish. They are tired of souls being lost without hearing the word of God in their heart language waiting for the fish to be cleaned.

> *"Behold, the days are coming," declares the Lord God, "when I will*
> *send a famine on the land — not a famine of bread, nor a thirst for*
> *water, but of hearing the words of the Lord. They shall wander*
> *from sea to sea, and from north to east; they shall run to and fro, to*
> *seek the word of the Lord, but they shall not find it."*[79]

MAST has quietly been gaining momentum, with the local church owning approximately one third of all active projects in Papua New Guinea and around forty percent of all worldwide projects.

There are a number of Bibles translated for newly created languages — languages that didn't previously exist. Some of these make sense. The Symbolic Universal Notation Bible was created for the deaf illiterate and deaf-blind that didn't previously have a written language. The process of teaching literacy in a language typically takes seven years in a school child. With the miracle of SUN, this has been reduced to mere weeks for deaf illiterate with no education. Praise the Lord! SUN makes sense and is bearing fruit, bringing people to Christ and growing churches.

Other new languages and their corresponding Bibles weren't intentional and unfortunately weren't isolated occurrences, but something that happens far too frequently. Teams are built with speakers from multiple languages (linguists may call them dialects), and in the process of translation the best word from the group of languages is used. This ends up with words from many languages, but a finished Bible that isn't a language anyone speaks because of the

---

[79] Amos 8:11-12

blending of languages like the Pahan Bible. This is terrible stewardship and has resulted in further poor stewardship, pouring money into developing scripture engagement programs for these made-up languages. This is also something that would not happen under local stewardship of His Word.

As the local church takes on Bible stewardship, the challenge western translators have of Scripture engagement ceases to be a problem. When the church owns and is engaged in the process from the first verse, there is no handoff of the Bible – the community is already engaged. A MAST workshop becomes an intensive Bible study, with believers deep in the Word full time for two weeks straight. This is about the same time in the Word as someone spending 15 minutes a day reading the Bible for a year.

As a strong proponent of discipleship to be the steward of God's Word in their heart language, the local church has excitement for this authority and responsibility. On the trip home from the Prayer Summit, I was drawn to the book of Zechariah. Some of the words in this chapter are hard truths. At the time the modern Bible translation movement started 100 years ago when Cameron Townsend made his trip to Latin America to sell Spanish Bibles to non-Spanish speakers, the local church did not exist as it does today. Today that church is strong and a transition from providing fish which creates long-term dependency to a process of teaching to catch and clean fish is long overdue.

I pray that the words in this chapter help remove the deception of the evil one. I prayed that prayer as I arrived in Papua New Guinea for the Prayer Summit and the Holy Spirit had me bursting out in laughter. As I've studied the Holy Spirit and Prayer, particularly the book *Possessing the Gates of the Enemy* (Jacobs, 2018), when prayer is answered, there will be that laughter. It doesn't mean the answer has happened on earth, but it has happened in the heavenlies and will happen on earth.

Chapter Twelve

These are the things that you shall do: Speak the truth to one another, render in your gates judgements that are true and make for peace[80]

I pray for this peace. Writing this book has given me the clarity that God developed Wycliffe Associates over the organization's 50 plus-year history to be disciple makers when it came to Bible translation. That's radically different from being an organization doing Bible translation. The results are stunning. The church is taking on the task as early proponents of Vision 2025 said would be necessary to complete the task. For the past five years, we've been preparing to disciple the church to become the steward, and we are on the cusp of explosive expansion of Bible translation. As churches start discipling other churches and translation teams independent from Wycliffe Associates and our traditional partners, we will see Vision 2025 come to fruition as it was envisioned over two decades ago.

---

[80] Zechariah 8:16

Chapter Thirteen – Faith of a Mustard Seed

At the recent Prayer Summits in Melanesia and Indonesia, our Pacific Prayer Coordinator Ginger led sessions on how to further engage the local church in praying for Bible translation. She shared the parable about faith the size of a mustard seed and handed out ribbon bookmarks with mustard seeds glued to them to the staff as reminders.

> *He said to them, "Because of your little faith. For truly, I say to you, if you have faith like a grain of mustard seed, you will say to this mountain, 'Move from here to there,' and it will move, and nothing will be impossible for you."* [81]

John, who was with us at these Prayer Summits with his wife Jean, has exercised tremendous faith over the years. Through that faith he has personally experienced every miracle in the Bible except seeing someone walk on water. I joke that I've done that one, but with my faith I wait until the water is in a solid state in the winter. Through the authority given to him by Jesus Christ, and in the name of Christ he has seen people raised from the dead, and countless healings including curing the deaf, dumb, and blind. Just as Jesus stretched out the hand of the cripple, John has seen Jesus through his prayer grow the leg of a man four inches.

God is in all of this. John shared a number of compelling stories at the Prayer Summits on the power of the Holy Spirit and the miracles that resulted as John prayed in the name of Jesus Christ. National team members were inspired by John's testimony and were drawn to seek

---

[81] Matthew 17:20

greater intimacy with the Holy Spirit and to exercise their faith in Jesus Christ as they move forward in their calling.

At our June Operations team meetings, the rest of our Operations team was stunned when I committed to starting 1200 language projects in the current fiscal year. This is roughly equivalent to the combined work of the three previous years for the entire organization. For the Pacific it will quadruple the number of active projects. I wasn't making this commitment in isolation. I was seeing God's hand accelerating translation across the Pacific and God providing the opportunity to open many gates, and I was stepping out with boldness in faith. Members of the team were hearing unprecedented numbers of languages God was calling us to equip the church. They affirmed these numbers as we met in December. God was using my faith to be bold and to encourage the team to also lead with boldness. As you see the God of miracles repeatedly do miracles, faith deepens.

> *I will surely gather all of you, Jacob;*
>> *I will surely bring together the remnant of Israel.*
> *I will bring them together like sheep in a pen,*
>> *like a flock in its pasture;*
>> *the place will throng with people.*
> *The One who breaks open the way will go up before them;*
>> *they will break through the gate and go out.*
> *Their King will pass through before them,*
>> *the Lord at their head.*[82]

One year from now, the local churches using MAST methodology should be managing the majority of Bible translation projects worldwide and discipling their scriptureless neighbors. Churches are

---

[82] Micah 2:12-13

already questioning the continued use of Western translators – they are recognizing that they have unintentionally outsourced their language.

As I've shared, particularly in Shakil's chapter, we are seeing churches planted, Muslims, Hindus, and Buddhists coming to Christ. Through our Deaf Ownership Translation and Symbolic Universal Notation Literacy programs we are witnessing deaf and deaf-blind coming to Christ. We also see God using rascals, terrorists, and prisoners as Bible translators. God is doing what He always does – using the unlikely to do the impossible.

> *But I received mercy for this reason, that in me, as the foremost, Jesus Christ might display his perfect patience as an example to those who were to believe in him for eternal life.*[83]

I clearly see my role now – not as the leader charging ahead, but as the servant and disciple maker anticipating the needs of the national leaders God has given to me to shepherd. God has built an amazing team that I have the honor of leading, and this book profiles only part of the team. There just aren't enough pages to tell the stories of servants of Christ like Domi and others that are doing incredible work for the Lord in this ministry.

When I took on the role leading to my present role 18 months ago, we had one active team in Indonesia, and no team, only one person, in Papua New Guinea. In the last 18 months we have seen the Papua New Guinea team be established and then multiply to four regional teams. We have seen the Indonesian team multiply to three regional teams, and each of these teams in both those countries are further multiplying to more teams as they subdivide the regions of Indonesia down towards a provincial level. The Papua New Guinea team is not only serving their nation and discipling to create these provincial teams

---

[83] 1 Timothy 1:16

within the regions, they are going out and helping build the teams in other Melanesian countries including Fiji, the Solomon Islands, and Vanuatu.

I can't do this. I'm not Melanesian. I don't speak any pidgin languages – be it Tok Pisin or Bislama, nor do I speak Indonesian or other Malay languages. None of these thousands of heart languages in the Pacific are my heart language. I can try to impart the vision of stewardship of God's Word. The national leaders on the Pacific team are far better equipped to tell their brothers and sisters in Christ: "We need to take responsibility and steward our languages." Personally, as part of the propagators of removing that stewardship and telling them they weren't capable of stewarding God's Word, my words ring hollow. The truth is being carried through these national leaders, whom I love, trust, and have the privilege of serving.

I pray over the next year the Melanesian team can be discipled to be the same disciple makers as the Papua New Guinea team. With that expertise, they will then be able to disciple and multiple within Melanesia and across to Polynesia and to the Australian aboriginal people. Much like the travels of the early apostles and disciples, we're going from island to island across the Pacific. As we move into Micronesia, it will likely be the Indonesian team that starts those efforts.

I mentioned early in the book of not feeling confident of my military leadership. As I was finishing the editing of this book, God drew me to Isaiah 41.

> *You whom I took from the ends of the earth,*
> *   and called from its farthest corners,*
> *saying to you, "You are my servant,*
> *   I have chosen you and not cast you off";*
> *fear not, for I am with you;*

be not dismayed, for I am your God;
I will strengthen you, I will help you,
  I will uphold you with my righteous right hand.
Behold, all who are incensed against you
  shall be put to shame and confounded;
those who strive against you
  shall be as nothing and shall perish.
You shall seek those who contend with you,
  but you shall not find them;
those who war against you
  shall be as nothing at all.
For I, the Lord your God,
  hold your right hand;
it is I who say to you, "Fear not,
  I am the one who helps you."[84]

As I read it, I clearly see God's five promises in verse 10. He is with me, He is my God, He will strengthen me, He will help me, and He will uphold me. With this, there is no reason to fear. The New International Version starts the first verse calling for silence from the islands. God has sent me to the islands of the Pacific. And he sends me without fear.

Today, God has me running the largest munitions plant in the world, forging the Sword of the Spirit in record numbers, and leading the fight against darkness in one of the darkest parts of the world. It's His anointing that has prepared me for this calling and season.

A prayer partner helped me see this recently in Fiji. As the two of us examined Ephesians 6, we read:

In all circumstances take up the shield of faith, with which you can
extinguish all the flaming darts of the evil one; and take the helmet

---

[84] Isaiah 41:9-13

of salvation, and the sword of the Spirit, which is the word of God, praying at all times in the Spirit, with all prayer and supplication. To that end, keep alert with all perseverance, making supplication for all the saints.[85]

The Sword of the Spirit is the word of God. In equipping the believers of the Pacific with Scripture in their heart language, we are forging many Swords of the Spirit. We are issuing these swords to saints of many nations that are trained warriors. Many of these warriors have been fighting since they were young children. As I visited the Ontenu village after the battle in the summer of 2018, young boys of perhaps six to eight years old were equipped with bows and death spears. By the time they become my age, they will have been trained warriors for half a century. Do you think Satan will take this changing sides of these warriors from darkness to light without a fight? Not a chance.

As saints fighting on the front line, we must be well equipped with the Sword of the Spirit. Psalm 91 is one Psalm that we need to keep near to our heart for protection. This was the Psalm that Satan twisted in his temptation of Jesus after His baptism.

He who dwells in the shelter of the Most High will abide in the shadow of the Almighty.
I will say to the Lord, "My refuge and my fortress, my God in whom I trust."
For he will deliver you from the snare of the fowler and from the deadly pestilence.
He will cover you with his pinions, and under his wings you will find refuge; his faithfulness is a shield and a buckler.
You will not fear the terror of the night, nor the arrow that flies by day,

---

[85] Ephesians 6:16-18

nor the pestilence that stalks in darkness, nor the destruction that wastes at noonday.

A thousand may fall at your side, ten thousand at your right hand, but it will not come near you.

You will only look with your eyes and see the recompense of the wicked.

Because you have made the Lord your dwelling place – the Most High, who is my refuge –

no evil shall be allowed to befall you, no plague come near your tent.

For he will command his angels concerning you to guard you in all your ways.

On their hands they will bear you up, lest you strike your foot against a stone.

You will tread on the lion and the adder; the young lion and the serpent you will trample underfoot.

"Because he holds fast to me in love, I will deliver him; I will protect him, because he knows my name.

When he calls to me, I will answer him; I will be with him in trouble; I will rescue him and honor him.

With long life I will satisfy him and show him my salvation."[86]

As I was in my morning quiet time preparing to travel between Papua New Guinea and Indonesia for the transition from the Melanesian Prayer Summit to the Indonesian Prayer Summit, I reflected on how three of the Papua New Guinea leaders are always brandishing their swords. Hardly a conversation or teaching goes by without scripture pouring forth from their tongues. They are rooted deep in the Word and have it in their hearts.

---

[86] Psalm 91

Later that morning I was in the hotel lobby talking to Kautum and Celsius, and David came down into the lobby. These were the three men that carry these well sharpened Swords of the Spirit I was contemplating. I pulled the three of them aside, and we talked about my observation, but more importantly, how critical it is to impart this same discipline across the team. If the Word of God is so valuable, how can we be ambassadors for it, if we don't have it stored in our hearts. We must be the light and the salt as we lead these battles for eternity across the Pacific.

Ephesians 6 then goes on to say that we must pray at all times in the Spirit. How can we pray in the Spirit if we don't know the Spirit? There's a reason God had me in a deep study of the Holy Spirit this past summer, preparing for the battles I will be commanding the team through.

God moved powerfully in this Prayer Summit as I wrapped up the editing of this book. My brother John and his wife Jean walked alongside me to mentor the team and help ensure the team is equipped. Surprisingly to me, but not to God, God used me to mentor John, but he does teach us that iron sharpens iron. I'd suspect as Paul discipled Timothy, there was a thing or two that Paul learned.

> *Iron sharpens iron,*
>   *and one man sharpens another.* [87]

We need the team to be fully functional Christians both baptized in water and baptized in the Holy Spirit. This is basic training for the team. Through the teaching, team members have stepped forward to move themselves from running on one or two cylinders to all four. Water baptism washes away the sins of the past.

---

[87] Proverbs 27:17

Chapter Thirteen

And now why do you wait? Rise and be baptized and wash away
your sins, calling on his name.[88]

Without baptism in the Spirit, how can we effectively pray in the Spirit as we're called in Ephesians 6:18?

With baptism in the Spirit we see two things, first gifts of the Spirit. Seldom does anyone get all the gifts, typically the body of Christ collectively has all the gifts of the Spirit, since the gifts are for the collective good of the body. These gifts can also be transitional – you get them for a specific need, then the gift ceases to be available.

To each is given the manifestation of the Spirit for the common
good. For to one is given through the Spirit the utterance of
wisdom, and to another the utterance of knowledge according to the
same Spirit, to another faith by the same Spirit, to another gifts of
healing by the one Spirit, to another the working of miracles, to
another prophecy, to another the ability to distinguish between
spirits, to another various kinds of tongues, to another the
interpretation of tongues. All these are empowered by one and the
same Spirit, who apportions to each one individually as he wills.[89]

The fruit of the Spirit is the second thing we see. Fruit takes time to ripen, as does the fruit of the Spirit. When the fruit is mature, all the characteristics of the fruit of the Spirit are present.

But the fruit of the Spirit is love, joy, peace, patience, kindness,
goodness, faithfulness, gentleness, self-control; against such things
there is no law.[90]

---

[88] Acts 22:16
[89] 1 Corinthians 12:7-11
[90] Galatians 5:22-23

While some would say that baptism in the Spirit isn't part of their doctrine, God tells us not to rely on man but on His Word.

> *You leave the commandment of God and hold to the tradition of men.*[91]

Throughout scripture we see the anointing of the Spirit. Sometimes we see this baptism in the Holy Spirit alongside baptism by water, sometimes preceding, and sometimes quite a bit later. What we do see with it is mighty power for the work of the Lord. As convicted as I am to the urgency of seeing Vision 2025 fulfilled, God has convicted me that the work cannot be done solely in the flesh, it can only be done by the leading of the Spirit.

In Papua New Guinea during our closing session we had a time of worship and communion. We also had a time of anointing. Several weeks ago, Koil had had a dream of Misson having a white butterfly land on his shoulder, symbolizing an anointing in the Spirit. Misson was one of many on the team that stepped forward for anointing by oil, and that night Koil had the same dream about Misson and the white butterfly symbolizing his anointing—one more saint running on all cylinders, properly anointed for the task ahead.

> *For all who are led by the Spirit of God are sons of God.*[92]

We're called to make supplication for all the saints. We know the battle they face. This book just touched on some of the stories of these battles. These aren't battles for today, these are battles for eternity. Many of my American readers won't have first-hand experience with the many miracles or spiritual warfare I describe, but it isn't a series of

---

[91] Mark 7:8
[92] Romans 8:14

coincidences. It is real. And eternal lives are at stake. These battles aren't without His protection.

> *If you walk in my statutes and observe my commandments and do them …You shall chase your enemies, and they shall fall before you by the sword. Five of you shall chase a hundred, and a hundred of you shall chase ten thousand, and your enemies shall fall before you by the sword.*[93]

I know two truths about my bride. I know the day is coming soon when she will be serving alongside me.

> *For the Lord God does nothing without revealing his secrets to his servants the prophets.*[94]

Until then, I know she spends countless hours in the war room in prayer and supplication for me, for the team I serve, for the thousands of translators we serve across the Pacific, and for their families, their tribes, and their nations. It is these prayers of Susan and thousands of other intercessors that lead to the mighty victories we are seeing.

I have two calls to action for you, my gentle reader. First, if you don't know Jesus Christ as your Lord and Savior, commit your life today. It's a simple process and costs us nothing, because Jesus Christ paid the price for our sins on the cross at Calvary. The rewards are eternal. There are three steps – recognize you are a sinner, believe that Jesus Christ died for your sins, and repent for your sins and turn your life over to Jesus Christ. You can do this by reciting the sinner's prayer, such as this one used by Billy Graham:

> *Dear Lord Jesus, I know that I am a sinner, and I ask for Your forgiveness. I believe You died for my sins and rose from the dead. I*

---

[93] Leviticus 26:3, 7-8
[94] Amos 3:6

turn from my sins and invite You to come into my heart and life. I want to trust and follow You as my Lord and Savior. In Your Name.

Amen.[95]

Second, we have a hard battle ahead of us for the next five years. This is the setup for Armageddon described in the book of Revelation. As soon as all have heard, Jesus will return. But Satan knows how the story ends and doesn't want to go down easy. I have seen many spiritual battles over the past five years, but only in the last month really had the full puzzle put together on the why of the intensity. In the field we need to be fully equipped with the full armor of God. At home, we need all of you praying without ceasing for the work. The work never ceases – the prayer needs to match. We are battling at the gates of the enemy. God has given us gates of our own to use in this work to equip and anoint the saints. The Glory of the Lord will shine as we win this battle and arm more saints with the Sword of the Spirit – that is the word of God. But we only get there through the prayer and supplication in the Spirit of many saints. God has given me an awesome group of committed Christians to lead and serve, but like any Army, it is the supply lines behind us – in this case those interceding for the front lines that brings victory.

> *In that day the Lord of hosts will be a crown of glory, … and strength to those who turn back the battle at the gate.*[96]

> *On this rock I will build my church, and the gates of Hell shall not prevail against it.*[97]

---

[95] https://peacewithgod.net/
[96] Isaiah 28:5-6
[97] Matthew 16:18

For the earth will be filled
with the knowledge of the glory of the Lord
as the waters cover the sea.[98]

You make known to me the path of life;
in your presence there is fullness of joy;
at your right hand are pleasures forevermore.[99]

---

[98] Habakkuk 2:14
[99] Psalm 16:11

Appendix One
A. W. Tozer Prayer of a Minor Prophet

O Lord, I have heard Thy voice and was afraid. Thou hast called me to an awesome task in a grave and perilous hour. Thou are about to shake all nations and the earth and also heaven, that the things that cannot be shaken may remain. O Lord, our Lord, Thou has stopped to honor me to be Thy servant. No man takes this honor upon himself save he that is called of God as was Aaron. Thou has ordained me Thy messenger to them that are stubborn of heart and hard of hearing. They have rejected Thee, the Master, and it is not to be expected that they will receive me, the servant.

My God, I shall not waste time deploring my weakness nor my unfittedness for the work. The responsibility is not mine but Thine. Thou hast said, "I knew thee—I ordained thee—I sanctified thee," and Thou has also said, "Thou shalt go to all that I shall send thee, and whatsoever I command thee thou shalt speak." Who am I to argue with Thee or to call into question Thy sovereign choice? The decision is not mine but Thine. So be it, Lord. Thy will, not mine, be done.

Well do I know, Thou God of the prophets and the apostles, that as long as I honor Thee Thou wilt honor me. Help me therefore to take this solemn vow to honor Thee in all my future life and labors, whether by gain or by loss, by life or by death, and then to keep that vow unbroken while I live.

It is time, O God, for Thee to work, for the enemy has entered into Thy pastures and the sheep are torn and scattered. And false shepherds abound who deny the danger and laugh at the perils which surround Thy flock. The sheep are deceived by these hirelings and follow them with touching loyalty while the wolf closes in to kill and destroy. I beseech Thee, give me sharp eyes to detect the presence of the enemy; give me understanding to distinguish the false friend from the true. Give me vision to see and courage to report what I see faithfully. Make my voice so like Thine own that even the sick sheep will recognize it and follow Thee.

Lord Jesus, I come to Thee for spiritual preparation. Lay Thy hand upon me. Anoint me with the oil of the New Testament prophet. Forbid that I should become a religious scribe and thus lose my prophetic calling. Save me from the curse that lies dark across the face of the modern clergy, the curse of compromise, of imitation, of professionalism. Save me from the error of judging a church by its size, its popularity or the amount of its yearly offering. Help me to remember that I am a prophet; not a promoter, not a religious manager—but a prophet. Let me never become a slave to crowds. Heal my soul of carnal ambitions and deliver me from the itch for publicity. Save me from the bondage to things. Let me not waste my days puttering around the house. Lay Thy terror upon me, O God, and drive me to the place of prayer where I may wrestle with principalities and powers and the rulers of the darkness of this world. Deliver me from overeating and late sleeping. Teach me self-discipline that I may be a good soldier of Jesus Christ.

I accept hard work and small rewards in this life. I ask for no easy place. I shall try to be blind to the little ways that I could make my life easier. If others seek the smoother path I shall try to take the hard way without judging them too harshly. I shall expect opposition and try to take it quietly when it comes. Or if, as sometimes it falleth out to Thy servants, I shall have grateful gifts pressed upon me by Thy kindly people, stand by me then and save me from the blight that often follows. Teach me to use whatever I receive in such manner that it will not injure my soul nor diminish my spiritual power. And if in Thy permissive providence honor should come to me from Thy church, let me not forget in that hour that I am unworthy of the least of Thy mercies, and that if men knew me as intimately as I know myself they would withhold their honors or bestow them upon others more worthy to receive them.

And now, O Lord of heaven and earth, I consecrate my remaining days to Thee; let them be many or few, as Thou wilt. Let me stand before the great or minister to the poor and lowly; that choice is not mine, and I would not influence it if I could. I am Thy servant to do Thy will, and that will is sweeter to me than position or riches or fame and I choose it above all things on earth or in heaven. Though I am chosen of Thee and honored by a high and holy calling, let me never forget that I am but a man of dust and ashes, a man with all the natural faults and passions that plague the race of men. I pray Thee therefore, my Lord and Redeemer, save me from myself and from all the injuries I may do myself while trying to be a blessing to others. Fill me with thy power by the Holy Spirit, and I will go in Thy strength and tell of Thy righteousness, even Thine only. I will spread abroad the message of redeeming love while my normal powers endure.

Then, dear Lord, when I am old and weary and too tired to go on, have a place ready for me above, and make me to be numbered with Thy saints in glory everlasting. Amen. (Dorsett, 2008)

Appendix Two – Reading List

Blackaby, Henry – *Experiencing God*

Chan, Francis – *Forgotten God*

DeYoung, Kevin – *Just Do Something*

Falkenstine, Mike – *Six Marks of a Disciple*

Goll, James W. – *The Lost Art of Intercession*

Goodwin, Roy; Roberts, Dave – *The Grace Outpouring*

Gruden, Wayne – *The Gift of Prophecy*

Heflin, Ruth Ward – *Glory*

Hernandez, David Diga – *Carriers of the Glory*

Herzog, David – *Glory Invasion*

Jeremiah, David – *The Spiritual Warfare Answer Book*

Joannes, David – *The Mind of a Missionary*

Laniak, Dr. Timothy S. – *When Shepherds Watch their Flocks*

Manning, Brennan – *The Ragamuffin Gospel*

Payne, Dr. Karl I. – *Spiritual Warfare*

Platt, David – *Follow Me*

Prince, Derek – *Spiritual Warfare for the End Times*

Qureshi, Nabeel – *Seeking Allah, Finding Jesus*

Ripkin, Nik – *Insanity of God*

Bibliography

Allender, D. (2010). *Sabbath: The Ancient Practices.* Thomas Nelson.

Challies, T. (2018, 12 11). *The 2019 Christian Reading Challenge.* Retrieved from challies.com: https://www.challies.com/resources/the-2019-christian-reading-challenge/

Creson, B. (2014). *The Finish Line.* Orlando: Wycliffe USA.

Crough, D., & Crough, D. (2007). *Eye to Eye, Heart to Heart: A Reflection on Wycliffe Bible Translators and Vision 2025.* Wycliffe Canada.

Dorsett, L. (2008). *A Passion for God: The Spiritual Journey of A. W. Tozer.* Chicago: Moody.

Fant, D. J. (1964). *A. W. Tozer: A Twentieth Century Prophet.* Christian Publications.

Godwin, R., & Roberts, D. (2012). *The Grace Outpouring: Becoming a People of Blessing.* David C. Cook.

Jacobs, C. (2018). *Possessing the Gates of the Enemy: A Training Manual for Militant Intercession.* Chosen Books.

Jeremiah, D. (2016). *The Spiritual Warfare Answerbook.* Thomas Nelson (June 14, 2016).

Mabury, P., Bentley, H., Fieldes, M., Ingram, J. I., & Daigle, L. (2015). First [Recorded by L. Daigle]. USA.

Pawson, D. (2007). *Unlocking the Bible.* HarperCollins Publishers.

Payne, K. (2011). *Spiritual Warfare: Christians, Demonization and Deliverance.* WND Books.

Prince, D. (2017). *Spiritual Warfare for the End Times.* Chosen Books.

Ripken, N., & Lewis, G. (2012). *Insanity of God.* B&H Books.

Sanders, J. O. (2007). *Spiritual Leadership: Principles of Excellence for Every Believer.* Chicago: Moody Publishers.

Smith, B. A. (2020). *Living Translation: Peace Children - The Sawi Story.* Xulon Press.

About the Author

Joe Gervais is the Pacific Regional Director for Wycliffe Associates, (www.wycliffeassociates.org) a ministry accelerating the work of Bible translation around the world. In his role as Pacific Regional Director, he serves on the front lines of Bible translation, directing partnerships, training, and support for churches and language groups across Indonesia, Melanesia, Micronesia, Oceania, and Polynesia. Joe lives in Arlington, Vermont, with his wife Susan and her mother Gladys. Joe and his wife have four sons, two daughters-in-law, three grandchildren, and one great-grandchild.

Made in the USA
Columbia, SC
12 January 2020